ENDORSEMENTS

Do you ever wonder [...] ife? At the end of your life, do y[...] done, good and faithful servant"? Do you want less stress and more joy in your life? Then this book is for you! Saturated with Scripture and engaging stories from his life on the mission field, Kyle shares practical wisdom that is rooted in deep, biblical theology. This is a book I heartily recommend to youth who want to know how they can be used of God in life and ministry, as well as to seasoned veteran pastors and missionaries who desire to finish well.

-JEFF DEMERLY, *ABWE Executive Director for Europe, the Middle East, and North Africa*

The Apostle Peter was clear in his writings of the importance of being reminded of sound Biblical truths. Thank you, Kyle, for following Peter's model in reminding your readers of the supreme importance of pursuing our walk with Jesus Christ as priority one. Any book that both challenges and convicts you regarding your walk with Christ is a worthy read. You are holding such a book in your hand. After 41 years of pastoral ministry it was a welcomed and needful reminder of cherishing and nourishing a God-centric life.

-JERRY PELFREY, *Lead Pastor in Mason, Ohio (1985-present)*

Once the initial excitement and the perceived glamour of ministry has past, those ministering need to be reminded of their source and their purpose. Kyle wonderfully establishes a basis for ministry, a basis that is centered on God and His Word. God is at work in us more than we are at work for Him. Missionaries need

Him more than God needs missionaries, and this truth will keep them effective in their chosen field of ministry. Kyle does a great job in reminding us all of these truths. This book is a much needed tool for all those seeking serve Him through sharing Christ with a lost and increasingly desperate world.

-Dr. Desmond Venter, *Grace Baptist Church, Amanzimtoti, South Africa*

Human hearts are tricky things. Knowing them and understanding them is a perpetual mystery to us. I find this to be true even of my own heart. In this book my friend Kyle Farran lays bare a portion of his heart so that we might be encouraged to examine the real source of the activity we call "service to God." The thesis of this book as expressed in its preface is that effective "ministry is not characterized by a busy schedule or an overflow of the will, but rather an overflow of the heart." Kyle has written from his heart's understanding of God's Word to help us examine our hearts closely. He gives us wisdom that flows from the experience of pursuing the development of a full and clean heart before God as the mainspring of life. I have watched him do this in the midst of the tension of ministry in multiple cultural settings. If you struggle to cooperate fully with God's molding ministry in your heart, read this book! It will help you! I know it helped me.

-Dr. Steve Stairs, *Pastoral Training Consultant for Africa, ABWE and fellow-wanderer in Hluhluwe Game Park*

Kyle has chosen a topic that is much needed and can be of great help to all Christian workers. Since he has had many contacts with missionaries, pastors, and others serving Christ, he is well qualified to understand the importance of spiritual health in serving the Savior. He has given many thoughts to encourage and challenge the reader. I have known Kyle since his call into the ministry, followed him in his missionary endeavors, and believe he fully understands the necessity of a long and fruitful ministry. He is not only an example but wants others to follow that example.

-ROBERT FARISON, *Pastor and Bible teacher*

Overflowing captures the essence of what it means for the Christian to want more of who God is and what He has to offer us. Not only does Kyle present a beautiful illustration of what living water looks like, he gives helpful and very practical tools for the Christian who is desiring to go deeper with God. Kyle uses the whole of Scripture to showcase the glory of God and how He wants to fully engage us in His incredible story. Really appreciate Kyle's heart as he shares his journey of ministry life and what God has done in and through him.

-RYAN CHRISTIAN, *Founder/President, Hideout Ministries*

Most books have a "must read" section. It may be a key sentence or paragraph that reveals the heart of the author or the main thrust of the work. I was looking for that as I started reading *Overflowing*. What surprised me was that as I read, I found paragraph after paragraph of helpful biblical material. This book supports those serving in ministry with material to assess and diagnose their soul, to reflect on where their strength for ministry comes from, and to examine inner thoughts and intentions. With the gentle honesty of someone who has been there, Kyle walks us through a thoroughly biblical examination of pride and humility, sin and holiness, joy and discouragement. Make no mistake: this is not a theological treatise on missions or ministry; it is a heart book designed for you and your ministry success.

-PAUL L. DAVIS, *President, ABWE International*

God has graciously captured Kyle's heart with the transforming realization that Gods ultimate goal is to display his amazing glory for all to see. He also touches the longing in us all to experience God's approval of our life and ministry at the end of our lives by hearing the Lord say "Well done". He joins these together by showing how we can receive the approval of God and bring much glory to him. Perhaps as valuable as anything is Kyle's incessant, repeating of God's great promise to always be searching for a heart that is fully given over to him (2 Chronicles 16:9) just so he can show himself strong through such a one!

-DREW WOODS, *pastor at Cement City Baptist Church, in Cement City, MI*

OVERFLOWING

MINISTRY AND MISSIONS THAT
FLOW FROM THE HEART

KYLE FARRAN

Carpenter's Son Publishing

Overflowing: Ministry and Missions That Flow from the Heart

© 2021 by Kyle Farran

Published by Carpenter's Son Publishing, Franklin, Tennessee

Published in association with Larry Carpenter of
Christian Book Services, LLC
www.christianbookservices.com

Author's note: Throughout this work, when Scriptures are shown, I italicize certain words or phrases for emphasis. These uses are mine, and the italics should not be considered part of the copyrighted text.

Edited by Bob Irvin

Cover design by Suzanne Lawing

Interior design by Suzanne Lawing

Printed in the United States of America

978-1-952025-77-8

To Heather,
my precious wife and best friend

CONTENTS

PART 4: THE OASIS – OVERFLOWING TO OTHERS

"Keep your heart with all vigilance,
for from it flow the springs of life."
Proverbs 4:23

Foreword

"What we do in life echoes in eternity!" This line from the lips of the Roman General Maximus in the epic historical film, *Gladiator*, was meant to inspire a legion of soldiers preparing for battle. It was intended to stir up courage and willingness to pour out their lives for the glory of Rome. There are many such causes people are willing to live and die for. But there is only one cause that truly does affect eternity—the cause of Christ. As Christians throughout the ages have known, our lives are not lived in vain. We will one day meet our dear Master and receive from him the reward for our service. This is what energizes us as servants of a worthy King.

The Apostle Paul told us, "For we must all appear before the judgment seat of Christ, so that each one may receive what is due for what he has done in the body, whether good or evil." The Greek word for "evil" that Paul uses is *phaulon*, a term that means "useless," and the opposite of "weighty." This is the motivation Christians draw on to fuel our service. We want our lives to be useful to Christ, to be weighty for him, and to leave an impression on eternity. We want to live lives of value and significance. We want to run the race in pursuit of pleasing our Lord. But with this holy pursuit comes the potential for unholy pitfalls. Are our motives pure? Do we employ means and methods that are glorifying to God? Do we attempt our tasks in our own strength for our own aggrandizement? Does our desire to be busy with kingdom work sometimes cause us to neglect other responsibilities God would have us attend to? These are the types of self-doubt that plague many missionaries, ministers, and church members. Is God more concerned by what we do... or who we are? Rather than seek the secret of success, we need to pause and ask, "What is the definition of success?"

In this helpful book Kyle Farran brings to bear on this topic his substantial experience on the mission field, his theological training, and his personal walk with the Lord. He guides us through the barren Savannah of self-doubt and burn-out to the lush oasis of usefulness and fulfillment in Christ. He will redirect our ambitions from output for the kingdom to realizing our dependence on input from our King. I found this book nourishing to my soul and a source of kindling for my motivation as a pastor and a Christian. I trust it will work wonders for you as you strive for the tender reassurance of the Master who says, "Well done, good and faithful servant."

-DR. CLINT ARCHER, *Senior Pastor, Christ Fellowship Baptist Church in Mobile, Alabama; weekly contributor for theCripplegate.com. Author of books on theology, missions, family, and Christian living*

Preface

The great weight of this work doesn't come from the human author, but from the "author of life" (Acts 3:15). For this reason, I would like to challenge you to intentionally read the verses listed in this book. Don't merely skim them. Be as the Bereans who "were more noble than those in Thessalonica; they received the word with all eagerness, examining the Scriptures daily to see if these things were so" (Acts 17:11). Set your heart to not merely understand my uninspired words, but to grasp the *inspired* Word of God. Be noble in your pursuit of understanding.

God is gracious to those who "set [their] heart to understand" (Daniel 10:12) His Word, which is a revelation of Himself. God promised Israel that "you will seek the Lord your God and you will find him *if* you search after him with all your heart and with all your soul" (Deuteronomy 4:29). The promise that we will find is only *if* we search in the prescribed way. And that is with all your heart and all your soul.

Pursue God by understanding His Word, keeping in mind this precious promise: "If you seek him, he will be found by you" (2 Chronicles 15:2).

Introduction

Years ago I discovered a tension in my life and ministry. Not a tension between other people, but a tension inside of me, the tension between being *still* and *busy*. Maybe you have felt it also. Because of my desire to hear God's "well done," I found myself busy *doing* for God. I desired to see God glorified through me, so I did and did and did.

I was addicted to busyness.

I would like to say I was trusting God for the results (because I felt I was), but my actions told a different story. One indication was I felt guilty whenever I stopped working. If I wasn't doing something, I felt I was being lazy, unproductive, and unfruitful. This caused me to fill every empty spot with something. You know the drill.

My life revealed what I really believed: that doing was the most important thing. I depended more on my actions for results than on *God's power*. If I was truly dependent on God for the results, I would have spent more time alone with Jesus, more time in prayer, and less time worrying about all the details while trying to "look busy."

I also desired a productive ministry. I *felt* productive when I was extremely busy—like I was so important to the ministry that I couldn't slow down. Since I was always doing something, surely all that activity was productive!

Unfortunately, busyness and productivity are not the same. I can finish my "to-do list" (and even reply to all my emails) yet accomplish nothing of spiritual worth! Yes, I am to be diligent in my labor like Paul. He "worked harder than any of them" (1 Corinthians 15:10), but there is a difference between being diligent and being addicted to busyness. I was the latter.

The other reason for my busyness was buried deep inside of me, and it took a lot of soul-searching to discover. The reason: pride. I was addicted to busyness because I wanted others to see me as significant. Significant people are busy people, right? Their work seems to be important. I felt that if I wasn't bouncing from task to task—like a six-year-old wired on coffee—I wasn't significant.

In our culture, "busy" has become synonymous with "significant." How do people describe an important person? "Oh, you know Bill. He is so busy!" In other words, if you are busy, everyone assumes your work is productive and you are significant. If you are busy for Jesus, then you must be super spiritual and doing important work—even if nothing supernatural is happening.

We all have a desire for significance and importance. When people ask us how we are doing, how do we reply? "Busy!" To which the other person gives an understanding, smug nod and says, "Yeah, me too." And we both walk away proud that we are doing something for God. Why? Because we are "busy for God."

But what if God is not impressed?

What if He wants something more?

As I was preparing for missions, God used a few books to shape my theology and heart. I learned through *Experiencing God*, by Henry Blackaby, that ministry wasn't about *me doing something for God*, it was about God doing something through me. I was joining God at work, not working for God.

The book *God's Passion for His Glory*, by John Piper and Jonathan Edwards, ignited my desire to glorify God in the greatest possible way. The desire to maximize the display of His glory has served as my compass ever since. It helped propel our family to minister to dying AIDS patients in South Africa. Just as a jeweler places a diamond on a black cloth to highlight its brilliance, God sends us to dark corners of the globe to put the brilliance of His glory on display. It was a joy to shine His light in such a dark place.

However, in the beginning I missed an important truth: Before God worked *through* me, He wanted to work *in* me. It took years to learn that ministry is not characterized by a busy schedule or an overflow of the will, but rather an overflow of the heart. You cannot minister from an empty cup.

I wrote this book for Christians actively involved in (or preparing for) ministry and missions. However, it's not just for those in full-time ministry, but also for those who have chosen to sacrificially serve the Lord with their time and resources. I invite you to join me in evaluating your life that you may "not run aimlessly" but instead hear "well done!" ringing in your ears for all eternity!

Get your free study guide here:
kylefarran.com/studyguide

Chapter 1

GOD'S HEART SEARCH

Why does God use some people more than others?

"For the eyes of the LORD run to and fro throughout the whole earth, to give strong support to those whose heart is blameless toward him" (2 CHRONICLES 16:9).

MY SEARCH FOR USEFULNESS

What do you long for in life and ministry?

My heart longs to bear spiritual fruit for the glory of God. I desire my life and ministry to be useful to God and count for eternity! My heart cries out with Moses when he says, "Let the favor of the Lord our God be upon us, and establish the work of our hands upon us; yes, establish the work of our hands!" (Psalm 90:17)

I don't want a wasted life. At the end of this age, with my life behind me and eternity before me, someone awaits. My Master. Entering His presence will be a moment I remember forever. His first words will ring in my ears for all eternity.

I long to hear: "Well done, good and faithful servant, enter into the joy of your master" (Matthew 25:21).

What do you desire to hear? Do you long to hear your Creator speak "well done" over your life? If so, how important is that to you?

For me, hearing "well done" is the pursuit of my life. Running well and pleasing my Master will be a source of unending joy. But this thought perplexed me: *What if I fail?* What if the life I thought was pleasing isn't actually pleasing to my Master? What if God says: "I had so much more I wanted to use you for. If only you had trusted me more." I don't want to get to Heaven and be surprised.

When first starting out in ministry, I didn't have a way to evaluate myself, so I tried the *run harder* approach. I felt being useful meant doing more by running harder. At first this approach seemed helpful because I could run harder. When we arrived in South Africa my wife and I spent the first three years learning Zulu and building relationships in the HIV/AIDS communities. Following this we spent ten months raising funds for the HIV/AIDS Care Home (and had our third child in the middle of this furlough). I then oversaw the building process and the hiring of workers, pushing as hard as I could to make the ministry work. Even if my body wasn't moving, my mind was. I was either going over Zulu words in my head or making ministry plans. Even when I was playing with my kids I was trying to learn Zulu words: *Ngiyagijima: I am running. Ngiyahamba: I am walking.* My mind and body were constantly going as hard as possible. The only time I was truly at rest was when we went to the game park or I was riding my motorcycle.

The week we opened the care home I began having debilitating migraines, which I later discovered were caused by stress. The same week, my wife came down with mononucleosis. This extreme fatigue forced us to temporarily close the care home soon after it opened.

I thought I was pleasing and being useful to God because I was running hard, but I was running too hard. I couldn't sustain the pace. Trying to run harder was impossible when I was already maxed out.

Striving to become useful to God by running harder and doing more led to two things. It led to uncertainty because I didn't know how much activity was enough. It also led to exhaustion because I didn't know how to set a manageable pace. It was impossible to slow down without feeling lazy or guilty that I wasn't doing more.

I still desire to run hard and minister to the best of my ability, but I don't want to burn out. Marathon runners don't sprint the whole race. Sprinting would cause them to collapse from exhaustion, and they would be unable to finish. At the same time, they don't go as slow as possible. Casually walking the race would be a failure. Finishing is not their only goal; they want to run well. They don't sprint, and they don't walk; they set a pace that is hard, but not too hard. One of the ways they do this is by checking their time at mile markers to ensure they're on pace to finish well. If they are falling behind, they adjust their pace.

That is what I want to do. Because of the potential to fail, I want a way to evaluate myself to see if I'm on course to be a servant who receives a "well done." If I'm off course, I would rather know now while adjustments can be made. With only one life to live, we need to adjust mid-race. There are no do-overs.

We don't need to simply run harder and hope for the best. Paul shows us a better way. It's true that we should work diligently because Paul tells us to "run that [we] may obtain" the prize (1 Corinthians 9:24). However, we should do more than just run hard. Paul also said that he did "not run aimlessly" (1 Corinthians 9:26). He was careful to run in the right direction.

Consider what would happen if a marathon runner ran his fastest 26.2 miles ever—but in the wrong direction! He would lose the race. Without clarity in our direction we run aimlessly without making progress toward our goal.

To find that direction, I asked myself a question:

Who will receive the "well done"?

Answer: *servants who are pleasing to God.* At the end of their lives, God will speak the words "Well done, good and faithful servant" over them (Matthew 25:21). God is only going to give a "well done" to useful servants. As God's children, we are pleasing to Him as His *child.* We become His children through salvation which is by grace alone, through faith alone without any works, and because of the merits of Christ alone. Paul writes: "For by grace you have been saved through faith. And this is not your own doing; it is the gift of God, not a result of works, so that no one may boast" (Ephesians 2:8, 9). After we become God's children through salvation, we have a responsibility to do the work He prepared for us. Paul continues: "For we are his workmanship, created in Christ Jesus for good works, which God prepared beforehand, that we should walk in them" (Ephesians 2:10). So the "well done" we are looking at here is for the "good and faithful servant." We are focusing on how we please God as His *servant.*

I then asked a follow-up question.

What kind of servant is pleasing to God?

Answer: *servants who are useful to accomplish His plan.* Masters want useful servants. No master is pleased with a useless servant. Paul highlights God's desire for useful servants when he says, "Therefore, if anyone cleanses himself from what is dishonorable, he will be a vessel for honorable use, set apart as holy, *useful to the master of the house,* ready for every good work" (2 Timothy 2:21). (Author's note: italicized uses in Scripture in this book are my emphasis and not part of the copyrighted text.) Think of God's servants in the past. They were useful to God in bringing about His plan which pleased God. If we can become like those useful servants, then we too can be pleasing to God.

This led me to the question that launched this book: *Why does God use some people more than others?*

Not every servant is equally useful to God. If I could understand what sets some people apart for God's use, I could know what areas of my life need the greatest growth. It could be like a mile marker to evaluate my life.

This book is born out of ten years meditating on this question. It is meant to help you evaluate your life that you may "not run aimlessly" but hear "well done" ringing in your ears for all eternity.

THE HEART

Throughout this book I talk a lot about my heart. When I do, I am not merely referring to the physical heart in my body. God's Word tells me that my heart is the core immaterial essence of who I am—my entire inner being that governs me. This includes my desires, intentions, emotions, will, and the source of my thoughts.[1] It touches everything I do, every decision I make, and every emotion I feel. It is "the entire internal dispositional complex that governs us."[2]

GOD'S SEARCH FOR USEFUL SERVANTS

My search led me to God's search for useful servants. For all the millions of people God could have used through history, He chose to use certain individuals instead of others. Why? Did the individuals have something in common that better prepared them to be used by God?

There were some who God chose to use in mighty ways. What did people like Enoch, Noah, Joseph, Moses, David, Daniel, and Isaiah have in common that set them apart? Was it their abilities, actions, or heart? Or was it simply God's sovereign choice, which had nothing to do with the individuals?

The answers to these questions have changed my life and ministry and are a continual guide to me. What at first seemed to be random character traits in biblical figures now fit seamlessly together. These traits are not just a list of more things to do; they form a picture of the person God wants us to be, the kind of man or woman best prepared to be used by God.

The answer to why God uses some people more than others is like a coin with two sides. On one side is God's sovereignty. On the flip side is man's responsibility.

SOVEREIGNTY

The first side of the coin is God's sovereignty. God chooses who He will bless and strengthen. "He chose David his servant and took him from the sheepfolds; from following the nursing ewes he brought him to shepherd Jacob his people, Israel his inheritance" (Psalm 78:70, 71). God has the right to choose *who* He uses and *how* He uses them.

God doesn't owe me anything. He is under no obligation to use me in accomplishing His plan. Because of this, my attitude should be one of humility. Like Isaiah, my heart should say, "O Lord, you are our Father; we are the clay, and you are our potter; we are all the work of your hand" (Isaiah 64:8). Unless God chooses to have His power work through me, I can do nothing. I have the same remarkable ability as a lump of clay . . . none.

Everything I have comes from God. "What do you have that you did not receive? If then you received it, why do you boast as if you did not receive it?" (1 Corinthians 4:7). This truth is both uplifting and humbling. It lifts me up to know that God gives me everything I need to be useful in life and ministry. It's also humbling to know I have no reason to be proud or rely on myself. At the end of the age, God will receive all the glory and praise because everything we have is a gift from Him. Even our crowns are symbols of the work God has done through us and will result in more praise for Him. "They cast their crowns before the throne, saying, 'Worthy are you, our Lord and God, to receive glory and honor and power, for you created all things, and by your will they existed and were created'" (Revelation 4:10, 11).

RESPONSIBILITY

The second side of the coin is my responsibility to submit to God and respond to His commands. Like the servant who was given five talents and then made five more, I am responsible to use what God gives me. I must "work out [my] own salvation with fear and trembling," but "it is God who works in [me], both to will and to work for his good pleasure" (Philippians 2:12, 13). I am unable to do or become anything in my own strength, but "I can do all things" through God's power (Philippians 4:13). The more open and receptive I am to His power at work in me, the more God will accomplish through me.

Because of this responsibility, God is looking for people who are responsive to Him.

These words changed my life: "For the eyes of the LORD run to and fro throughout the whole earth, to give strong support to those whose heart is blameless toward him" (2 Chronicles 16:9).

There are three truths about God in this passage that have changed how I seek to please God: God is conducting a search, God gives strong support, and God supports those whose heart is completely His.

1. God is conducting a search.

"For the eyes of the LORD run to and fro throughout the whole earth" (2 Chronicles 16:9).

Back and forth, back and forth. God is searching the world for a certain kind of person. In the description of God's search, it seems as though this kind of person is, sadly, not very common. When God was searching for someone to shepherd His people, He found David. There wasn't a list of people who would all prove a good fit—just David. Even more startling is how God spoke about Job. God said of Job that there was no one else like him on earth (Job 1:8). God saw something different in David and Job, something that set them apart from everyone else.

If the only factor in who God chooses to use is His sovereignty, He wouldn't need to search. He wouldn't need to test hearts. He could simply choose without regard to the person and then infuse them with everything they need. There is an important distinction between God's choice of who He uses in ministry and God's choice in election unto salvation. In election "he chose us in him before the foundation of the world" (Ephesians 1:4), before we were "born and had done nothing either good or bad" (Romans 9:10). So, we are not looking at that choice. God's choice in election was before we were alive. *This* search, and choice, is while we are alive.

Even though God is looking at our hearts, He doesn't choose us because of our personal greatness. If that were true, we would have reason to be proud. He is looking for something different. The next chapters in this book will unpack this in more detail.

Because God's plan on earth is not complete, His search is not over. God is looking. The idea may strike you as simple, but let it really sink in. *God is looking.* The Creator of the universe is searching the world for people to use for His glory.

As we consider God's search, I believe it is important to clarify what is not being said. The fact that God is searching does not mean that He is passively waiting for us to become the right kind of person in our own strength. Rather, while God is searching our hearts moment by moment He is also working to conform us to His image. God is actively at work in our heart, enabling all growth in Christlikeness and holiness. In this book I have chosen to focus more on God's search of our hearts, but these truths exist side by side: God is searching and God is working.

The fact that God is searching also does not mean that He lacks knowledge or that He doesn't know what He will find. When I search for something, it is because I don't know where to find it. God is all-knowing and everywhere present. He knows all that is and will be. Not only does He know all that will be, He is sovereignly in control of all that comes to pass. When God finds what He is searching for, He is finding a work of His own hand. He is searching for hearts that are ready for His purpose.

Like an orchard farmer nourishes and prunes the trees to help them produce, God works in us to make us grow. Just as an orchard farmer searches his own trees to see if the fruit is ripe, God is searching us. He is not wandering through random fields hoping to find fruit. He is searching His field. He is searching us, inspecting us, and waiting for us to mature so we can be ready for His purpose.

This makes the impact of God's search even more powerful. God is searching, working, all-knowing, and all-powerful. He is at work in us, around us and through us. As He works, He is looking for people to bring about His perfect plan. And He is not just looking for willing people. There is a certain kind of person "to whom [he] will look" (Isaiah 66:2).

What excited me was this thought: *I could become the kind of person to whom God looks.*

This became my consuming desire: to become one to whom God looks. Not that my behavior would guarantee that God would use me as I planned, but that I would be ready for whatever task He chose to set before this lump of clay.

If God is truly searching for people to use for His glory, then surely this would be scattered through His Word. As I looked, that is just what I found! God is conducting a search. As you read these verses, picture God speaking these words about you.

GOD'S HEART SEARCH

(Author's note; once more as a reminder: italics are mine and added for emphasis.)

"The LORD has sought out a man after his own heart" (1 Samuel 13:14).

"But the LORD said to Samuel, 'Do not look on his appearance or on the height of his stature, because I have rejected him. *For the LORD sees not as man sees:* man looks on the outward appearance, but *the LORD looks on the heart'"* (1 Samuel 16:7).

"And you, Solomon my son, know the God of your father and *serve him with a whole heart and with a willing mind, for the LORD searches all hearts* and understands every plan and thought. If you seek him, he will be found by you, but if you forsake him, he will cast you off forever" (1 Chronicles 28:9).

"Behold, *the eye of the LORD is on those who fear him,* on those who hope in his steadfast love" (Psalm 33:18).

"For though the LORD is high, *he regards the lowly,* but the haughty he knows from afar" (Psalm 138:6).

"All these things my hand has made, and so all these things came to be, declares the LORD. *But this is the one to whom I will look:* he who is humble and contrite in spirit and trembles at my word" (Isaiah 66:2).

"The LORD searches the heart and tests the mind, to give every man according to his ways, according to the fruit of his deeds" (Jeremiah 17:10).

"O great and mighty God, whose name is the LORD of hosts, great in counsel and mighty in deed, whose eyes are open to all the ways of the children of man, rewarding each one according to his ways and according to the fruit of his deeds" (Jeremiah 32:18, 19).

"So it was until the days of David, *who found favor in the sight of God* and asked to find a dwelling place for the God of Jacob" (Acts 7:45, 46).

"[H]e raised up David to be their king, of whom he testified and said, *'I have found in David the son of Jesse a man after my heart,* who will do all my will'" (Acts 13:22).

"By faith Enoch was taken up so that he should not see death, and he was not found, because God had taken him. Now *before he was taken he was commended as having pleased God.* And without faith it is impossible to please him, for whoever would draw near to God must believe that he exists and that he rewards those who seek him" (Hebrews 11:5, 6).

"For the eyes of the Lord are on the righteous, and his ears are open to their prayer. But the face of the Lord is against those who do evil" (1 Peter 3:12).

The God who holds the universe in His hands is searching the world for men and women pleasing to Him. He is searching my heart and your heart. The reason this is so important is because of what God does with those He finds. When God finds the kind of heart that pleases Him, He pours out His strong support on their life.

It's amazing that we can become people who are pleasing to God!

God is looking. Right now. Today. Will you be found by God as pleasing to Him?

2. God gives strong support (strength) to those He finds.

" . . . to give strong support" (2 Chronicles 16:9).

The God who is "able to do far more abundantly than all that we ask or think, according to the power at work within us" is searching for people He can empower and use to bring about His plan (Ephesians 3:20).

He is waiting with power!

I don't know about you, but I need strong support! Christ revealed how weak I am when He said, "Apart from me you can do nothing" (John 15:5). Without His support, all my efforts, all my labors for the spread of the gospel, will never make a difference. I long to have a life that is used by God and bears much fruit, but I can't do it in my own strength. I desperately need His power. Apart from Him, I can do nothing.

When we look at the descriptions of when God used His people, success was always contingent on His power. God's special favor on individuals is described in a few different ways. In these verses, notice the reason *why* these people succeeded.

The Lord was with them:

"But *the Lord was with Joseph* and showed him steadfast love and gave him favor in the sight of the keeper of the prison" (Genesis 39:21).

"And David had success in all his undertakings, *for the Lord was with him*" (1 Samuel 18:14).

"And David became greater and greater, *for the Lord, the God of hosts, was with him*" (2 Samuel 5:10).

The Lord gave victory:

"And *the Lord gave victory* to David wherever he went" (2 Samuel 8:6).

The eye of God was on them:
"But *the eye of their God was on the elders of the Jews*, and they did not stop them until the report should reach Darius and then an answer be returned by letter concerning it" (Ezra 5:5).

The hand of God was on them:
"For on the first day of the first month he began to go up from Babylonia, and on the first day of the fifth month he came to Jerusalem, *for the good hand of his God was on him*. For Ezra had set his heart to study the Law of the Lord, and to do it and to teach his statutes and rules in Israel" (Ezra 7:9, 10).

"I took courage, *for the hand of the Lord my God was on me*, and I gathered leading men from Israel to go up with me" (Ezra 7:28).

"*The hand of our God was on us*, and he delivered us from the hand of the enemy and from ambushes by the way" (Ezra 8:31).

"And I told them of *the hand of my God that had been upon me for good*" (Nehemiah 2:18).

The Lord made them prosper:
"Then I replied to them, '*The God of heaven will make us prosper,* and we his servants will arise and build, but you have no portion or right or claim in Jerusalem'" (Nehemiah 2:20).

The Lord gave favor and compassion:
"*And God gave Daniel favor and compassion* in the sight of the chief of the eunuchs" (Daniel 1:9).

The Lord was with them:
"No man shall be able to stand before you all the days of your life. Just as I was with Moses, so *I will be with you*" (Joshua 1:5).

"*The Lord is with you* while you are with him. If you seek him, he will be found by you, but if you forsake him, he will forsake you" (2 Chronicles 15:2).

They succeeded because God gave them strong support!

God's power accompanies His presence. When Moses spoke to God, notice the relationship between God's favor and His presence:

"And he said to him, 'If your presence will not go with me, do not bring us up from here. For how shall it be known that I have found favor in your sight, I and your people? Is it not in your going with us, so that we are distinct, I and your people, from every other people on the face of the earth?' And the Lord said to Moses, 'This very thing that you have spoken I will do, for you have found favor in my sight, and I know you by name'" (Exodus 33:15-17).

When our life and ministry find favor with God, He gives us more of His presence. The sign of God's favor is not the absence of problems, but rather more of His presence as He goes with us. As New Testament Christians, we never lose the presence of the indwelling Holy Spirit. Christ told us: "I am with you always, to the end of the age" (Matthew 28:20). However, just as water can be present as a trickle or a torrent, we can have more or less of God's presence in our life.

God's strong support allows us to succeed in the work He calls us to do. But ministry "success" does not always mean that our personal ministry plans are accomplished. Our ministry plans might even fail! True ministry success means that *God's will* is accomplished and, by trusting in God, we glorify Him. Even while sitting in prison Paul was a recipient of God's strong support. God was blessing the spread of the gospel in His time; Satan had not defeated Paul.

However, God doesn't give this strong support to everyone. He reserves it for certain individuals.

3. God supports those whose heart is completely his.

" . . . to those whose heart is blameless toward him" (2 Chronicles 16:9).

The English Standard Version also notes that the word "blameless" can be translated as "whole." This is someone whose heart is whole toward God, one with an undivided heart. The New American Standard Bible translates this verse as "those whose heart is completely His."

When God searches, He is looking for a servant after His own heart.

God is looking at hearts. He is searching for men and women who are pleasing to Him. He is not looking at our accomplishments, appearance, eloquence, or abilities. He is looking at the heart.

God is interested in who we are, not what we can do for Him. This is because it is God who does all the work through us.

Here is a thrilling thought: no one is more qualified to be used by God than anyone else.

There are no unfair advantages. What set David apart was his heart. The qualification for being pleasing to God is not an ability but a state of the heart. All of God's children can become pleasing to Him. We can be a person to whom God looks, not because of great things we do, but because of a heart that pleases God.

Because of this, my daily goal is no longer to accomplish great things for God. It is to become the kind of person He wants me to be. As I do, He will fill me with more of His power to accomplish the work He desires!

God tells us that He is looking for a certain kind of person on whom to pour out His strength. Let's make it our aim to become that person!

Contrary to popular opinion, doing more for God isn't what God notices. God looks first at your *being*, not your *doing*.

He is looking at your heart.

Chapter 2

OVERFLOWING HEARTS

What kind of heart are my actions flowing from?

*"Keep your heart with all vigilance, for from it
flow the springs of life"* (PROVERBS 4:23).

WHO YOU ARE: YOUR HEART

Our heart is the most important part about us because that is
where God is looking. The reason God looks at our heart: actions
flow from that center of our being. To say it a different way, our
doing flows from our being. Who you are (your heart) is more
important than what you do (your actions), because what you do
flows out of who you are. This is the central theme of this book.

If you remember nothing else from this book, remember this:
*Who you are is more important than what you do, because what
you do flows out of who you are.*

To ensure clarity, let's consider what is not being said. I am
not saying that what you do is insignificant. What you do is very
important, but who you are is *more* important. The reason is be-

cause your actions (what you do) must flow from a right heart (who you are).

If the well is sweet, so is the water that is drawn from it. The opposite is also true: if the well is bitter, so is the water drawn from it. For this reason, Solomon's proverb from the start of this chapter reminds us that our primary focus must be our heart: "Keep your heart with all vigilance, for from it flow the springs of life."

My passion is to see your service to God in ministry become an overflow of the heart, not an overflow of a busy schedule. For this to happen, your heart must be the central focus of your life and ministry. God must fill your heart to the point that His life and power overflow into all you do.

God doesn't just want my actions; He also wants my heart. He wants all of me.

USEFUL VESSELS

God is looking for useful servants. But just because I am a willing servant doesn't mean I'm useful. God is not merely looking for willing people who work hard. As servants of God, there are degrees of usefulness. Some servants' hearts are more useful than others. Consider the apostle Paul's words to Timothy.

> "Now in a great house there are not only vessels of gold and silver but also of wood and clay, some for honorable use, some for dishonorable. Therefore, *if* anyone cleanses himself from what is dishonorable, he will be a vessel for honorable use, set apart as holy, useful to the master of the house, ready for every good work" (2 Timothy 2:20, 21).

Did you notice the "if" I chose to highlight? Usefulness is contingent. My heart influences my usefulness to God. This is not to say that God is somehow limited in how He uses me. God uses me every day despite my sinfulness and brokenness. I will never be a perfect vessel on this side of eternity, but, at the same time, this passage is very clear: the state of my heart influences *how* the Master will use me.

God uses all of His children, but He uses us in different ways. The NIV translation says it like this: "some are for special purposes and some for common use" (2 Timothy 2:20). This doesn't mean that the common tasks are unimportant! Daily faithfulness in common tasks prepares me for the uncommon. I must be faithful in little tasks before God will entrust me with big ones. As God refines me, I will become more useful for "honorable" and "special" purposes.

What kind of service do you want to be used for? Do you want to be a vessel of "wood and clay" or one of "gold and silver"?

These verses have awakened in me a deep longing to be both pleasing and "useful to the master" (2 Timothy 2:20). However, to be the first, I must be the second. No master is pleased with a useless servant. Therefore, I need to know how to live in a way that is "useful to the master." Being useful to the master is the mile marker I use to evaluate my life. If I am growing in usefulness to God, my life will be pleasing to Him.

It's important to note that being used by God is not a fast and easy road. Consider some of the great biblical heroes mentioned already: Noah, Joseph, Moses, David, Daniel. They didn't take the fast road to being used by God, nor the easy one. They didn't "name it and claim it." They endured many trials and setbacks. God's plan took years to unfold. At many points in their life it probably didn't look like they were a chosen instrument of God. Things were not going well. However, God was first at work in them and around them before He worked through them.

God works on His eternal timetable, not ours. Being used by God is usually a hard road, but it leads to a great destination. As missionary Jim Elliot said: "He is no fool who gives what he cannot keep to gain what he cannot lose."[3] Being used by God is worth the wait and the cost.

If you want to be someone to whom God looks—one who receives God's "strong support," His "well done," and is "useful to the Master"—it comes down to your heart.

OVERFLOWING HEARTS

We had the privilege of living one hour from the Hluhluwe Imfolozi Game Park in South Africa, the oldest proclaimed nature reserve in Africa. Living so close allowed us to regularly visit the park on weekends. One day, just before sunrise, we began driving through the park. It was still too dark to distinguish trees from elephants or rocks from lions. Many vehicles were driving slowly in the pre-dawn hours, straining to see animals through the shadows. Not us. We didn't waste time with shadows. I drove at a steady pace because I wanted to be somewhere at daybreak. The river. We had learned this is the best place to see animals. The animals need the river's water to survive, and every morning at first light they come from miles around to quench their thirst. This morning was no different. We rolled to a stop at the river as the sun peeked over the horizon, turning the landscape golden. As the water shimmered in the early morning sunbeams, animals of all kinds came to drink. We spent the next hour sipping our coffee while watching rhinos, zebras, impala, giraffes, lions, and elephants all come to drink their fill. One thing is true of all game parks: water is needed for life. Without it, the animals will die.

Another incredibly unique African game park is in the Okavango Delta. Located above South Africa in the country of Botswana, the Moremi Game Reserve in the Okavango Delta is unlike any other. What makes the Okavango unique is its location. It is created by a river that literally ends in the desert, never reaching the ocean or sea. Each year the river floods and creates an amazing, lush grassland where animals migrate to find food and refreshment. But this isn't just a nice watering hole in the desert. Each year the water spreads up to 5,800 square miles (15,000 square kilometers), roughly the size of Connecticut.[4] Elephants, buffaloes, giraffes, hippos, antelope, leopards, hyenas, zebras, crocodiles, and 482 species of birds make the delta their home.[5] Like an oasis in the desert, the Okavango's overflow gives life to all the animals. Life exists because of this river.

What do water and rivers have to do with us?

The reason a river is useful is because it allows water to flow to far places. That is the river's purpose. A dry river or streambed is not useful. In the Okavango Delta, the river overflows its banks spreading life-giving water to all it touches.

God's purpose is to use us like an overflowing stream. It is what makes us useful. For us to be useful, God wants to fill our heart and overflow to others.

In the remaining chapters we'll take an in-depth look at the kind of heart that is useful and pleasing to God, the kind He loves to fill to overflowing. Comparing our life to an overflowing stream, we will examine the different aspects of our heart that please God. My prayer is that your heart will be filled to overflowing and become a heart that catches God's eye.

The illustration of an overflowing stream has four parts. I will use these to provide the structure for the rest of this book: the spring, the stream, the barriers, and the oasis. In each part, the chapters will unpack the truths you can apply to your heart to become more useful to God. An overflowing life and ministry only happen when we faithfully apply the truths from each part.

1. The Spring

A spring is where water that has been flowing underground emerges aboveground. Some springs are fed by an underground river or stream. Day after day a spring pours out clean, unpolluted water.

For us, life is all about the spring which is the fountain of life. God is that eternal spring and the "fountain of living waters" (Jeremiah 2:13). He is the source of our temporal physical life and eternal spiritual life.

He alone is the source of all good, and He alone deserves the glory. Because of this, we exist to magnify Him.

2. The Stream

The stream will become a dry bed of rocks unless it stays connected to the spring. We are like the streambed. By ourselves, we are empty and have nothing to offer. As Jesus said: "Apart from me you can do nothing" (John 15:5).

When our life is connected to the spring, His life-giving water flows through us. This is where our strength to minister to others comes from. Only when we connect with God and depend on His power will our ministry result in true spiritual change. We must stay connected to the spring, our source of life.

3. The Barriers

What happens when barriers block the entrance to the stream? The water is dammed up and stops flowing. When we allow sin in our life, the net result is something like throwing rocks and trash into the mouth of a stream. They hinder water from flowing. Spiritually, this sin hinders us and we either become a dry streambed or one with only a small trickle of water.

Are we allowing—or hindering—God to flow through us? If we're allowing sin to remain in our life, even small sins, we're hindering God's power from flowing through us.

If God is not flowing through us, it may be because we've allowed barriers of sin to get in the way. Like water, God is searching for hearts that have the barriers of sin removed and are open to Him. "For the eyes of the Lord roam throughout the earth, so that He may strongly support those whose heart is completely His" (2 Chronicles 16:9, NASB).

God is searching. Does He find openness or barriers in your heart? My heart?

4. The Oasis

The Okavango Delta is an oasis in the desert, an area that provides water for countless animals in the middle of barrenness. That is what our life is like when we are filled to overflowing. This world is like a desert for people's souls. We can become like a desert oasis that shares life-giving water. Others seek us to find refreshment and life for their weary souls because they see something different in us. They see an overflow of joy in God. When people are hurting and broken, we can be there to point them to the spring of living water.

When we are filled to overflowing we will become like an oasis in the desert.

An overflowing life is possible because the "fountain of living waters" is waiting to flow through us!

To start our in-depth look at our heart, we must travel with the spring's current.

Part 1:

THE SPRING - TRAVELING WITH THE CURRENT

Growing up as a missionary kid in Papua New Guinea, one of my favorite things to do was go to the river. My friends and I would jump off cliffs, float down the river using inner tubes or fallen banana trees, or relax on sandbars. I greatly anticipated the day when I could go to the river without adult supervision. It wasn't a raging river, but it was swift and had fallen trees where you could get trapped underwater.

Being a strong swimmer was important, but even more important was learning to travel with the current. In a lake or pool, you can swim where you want. There is no current pulling you any specific direction. In a river, you must travel with the current. You swim, but you are swimming in the direction that the current takes you. You never swim straight across a river, you swim at an angle to reach the side. If you fight the current, you get exhausted and could drown. If you learn to travel with the current, swimming seems almost effortless because you are traveling where the river is going.

When we are not traveling with the current of God's plan, we are like a swimmer who is trying to go against the current and set our own direction. It's like constantly fighting against His plan. God wants to use servants who travel with Him and His plan, not those who are fighting. He wants servants content to travel in the current of His will. These are the servants most useful to Him, the ones who will travel far with Him.

To be useful to God we must travel with the current of His heart. This begins with understanding *who God is* and *what He desires.*

Chapter 3

THE SPRING

Am I pursuing the same goal as God?

"I have found in David the son of Jesse a man after my heart"
(ACTS 13:22).

WHAT IS THE SPRING?

God is like an eternal spring—the source and fountain of life. Like a spring that constantly pours out pure water day after day, everything we are and have flows from God. "'Who has given a gift to him that he might be repaid?' For from him and through him and to him are all things. To him be glory forever. Amen" (Romans 11:35, 36). From His unlimited goodness He is constantly overflowing.

He is the source of our life, now and forever. He alone is the source of all good and He alone deserves all glory. Because of this, we exist to magnify Him.

David expresses this truth:

"Blessed are you, O LORD, the God of Israel our father, forever and ever. Yours, O LORD, is the greatness and the power and the glory and the victory and the majesty, for all that is in the heavens and in the earth is yours. Yours is the kingdom, O LORD, and you are exalted as head above all. Both riches and honor come from you, and you rule over all. In your hand are power and might, and in your hand it is to make great and to give strength to all. And now we thank you, our God, and praise your glorious name. But who am I, and what is my people, that we should be able thus to offer willingly? For all things come from you, and of your own have we given you" (1 Chronicles 29:10-14).

Everything we have comes from God's hand. Every breath. Every heartbeat. Every dollar. Every meal. It's all a gift. The New American Standard Bible paints the picture well with this verse: "from Your hand we have given You" (1 Chronicles 29:14). We take from His hand and give back to Him. When we serve or give to God we are simply returning what He first gave us.

God is the sum of all beauty, excellence, and worth. This makes Him the great and precious treasure of the universe. For "whom have I in heaven but you? And there is nothing on earth that I desire besides you" (Psalm 73:25). God did not create the universe or mankind out of need, for "he himself gives to all mankind life and breath and everything" (Acts 17:25). He created from the overflow of His supreme and infinite delight in Himself that He might display His glory. "For my own sake, for my own sake, I do it, for how should my name be profaned? My glory I will not give to another" (Isaiah 48:11).

As God acts for His glory He allows people to see and delight in His excellence. The desire and delight of our heart will be to see more of His glory. Our heart will forever cry: "One thing have I asked of the Lord, that will I seek after: that I may dwell in the house of the Lord all the days of my life, to gaze upon the beauty of the Lord and to inquire in his temple" (Psalm 27:4). Seeing His glory will result in the never-ending, ever-increasing joy of His people.

God is our spring and fountain.

WHY DOES TRAVELING WITH THE CURRENT MATTER TO US?

My goal is to please God, hear "well done," and receive my eternal reward.

If these are your goals also, it begs this question: how do you achieve these things?

It isn't by doing what you think is best. Instead, it's by aligning your goal to God's goal. Your goal is connected to his. Like swimming in a river, your goal is to swim where the current will take you. This doesn't mean your goal isn't met. When you serve as God desires, it results in accomplishing your goals of pleasing Him, hearing "well done," and receiving eternal reward.

Traveling with the current means aligning with God and His desires. It is not fighting the current but rather submitting to it and actively working with it to go in the same direction and to the same destination. To illustrate how important this is, imagine you are a server at a restaurant.

As a server, your goal is to receive a "well done" from those you serve, either by their complimenting you in front of your manager or, preferably, by a large tip. (Or both!) How would you pursue that goal? When someone places an order, their desire becomes your desire. If they desire a steak, your desire is to bring them the best steak possible, just as they ordered it. Your goal of a tip is contingent on aligning your goal to their goal.

What would happen if you brought something they didn't order? Perhaps a plate of oysters instead of that steak? Not only would the customer's goal not be met, neither would yours. Even if you carefully prepared the oysters because you thought they were better than steak, this wouldn't help. Your effort doesn't change what the customer wants.

Effort doesn't count if it's not aligned with God's goals and desires. You need to know what God ordered. To please God, you need to pursue His desires. If you don't align yourself with God's desires then your service and sacrifice will be met with the same response Saul received: "Has the Lord as great delight in burnt offerings and sacrifices as in obeying the voice of the Lord? Behold, to obey is better than sacrifice" (1 Samuel 15:22). You can serve and sacrifice your entire life, but if you are not aligned to God's desires the only person you are pleasing is yourself. Aligning with God by traveling with the current is essential to pleasing God.

WHY DOES TRAVELING WITH THE CURRENT MATTER TO GOD?

What kind of servant does a king desire?

Imagine a king who sent his servant as a representative (ambassador) to a foreign land, and the servant did whatever he wanted. The king gave specific goals he wanted accomplished, but the servant disregarded them. The servant worked hard, but he made absolutely no progress on the king's goals.

Because the servant was not aligned to the king's goals, he wasn't serving the king. He was fulfilling his own desires, not the king's. Like Cain in the Bible, he served according to his plan, not God's command.

Would this servant be honoring the king? No. By not aligning he makes the king look incompetent and unworthy of being followed. The servant says he wants to please the king, but he wants to do it *his* way. He is an unsubmitted servant.

The king would rather send a different servant whose behavior wouldn't sabotage the king's goals. In the same way, God wants servants who are aligned with Him. He wants servants who travel with His current toward His goal.

This illustration—the king and his servant—will be used throughout this book. Each time focuses on a *different* way that God's glory is helped or hindered by the kind of servant we are. Picture yourself as the servant and consider how your life either helps or hinders God's glory from being seen.

HOW DO WE TRAVEL WITH GOD'S CURRENT?

In order to align ourselves to God by pursuing His goals and desires, we must understand God's heart. It's a vital question: *what does God's heart desire?*

Growing up I knew I was supposed to do everything for God's glory. "So, whether you eat or drink, or whatever you do, do all to the glory of God" (1 Corinthians 10:31). But somehow I had missed this truth: not only is it right for me to do everything for God's glory, it is also right for God to do everything for God's glory! The book *God's Passion for His Glory* shook my world. I had always seen God as being, first of all, for man. After all, He died for sinners so that we could be with Him forever, right? In the book, author John Piper uses a famous essay written by Jonathan Edwards that showed through Scripture that God is indeed for man—just not as I had assumed. God is for man by first being *for Himself*. As He acts for Himself to display His glory, man receives what is best for him or her—more of God, our eternally satisfying treasure.

It's for my good that God exalts Himself! I used to think God loved me by making much of me (showing how valuable I was by dying for me). And while He does love me, mankind is not the center of the universe. God is.

God's ultimate goal in all He does is *His* glory. He wants to put His glory on display to be seen and delighted in. Remember this vital verse? "For my own sake, for my own sake, I do it, for how should my name be profaned? My glory I will not give to another" (Isaiah 48:11).

This is the heart of God.

Here are a few ways that God acts for His glory.

We were created for His glory.

"Everyone who is called by my name, whom I created for my glory, whom I formed and made" (Isaiah 43:7).

"He is the image of the invisible God, the firstborn of all creation. For by him all things were created, in heaven and on earth, visible and invisible, whether thrones or dominions or rulers or authorities—all things were created through him and for him" (Colossians 1:15, 16).

God redeemed Israel for His glory.

"For the LORD has redeemed Jacob, and will be glorified in Israel" (Isaiah 44:23).

God saved Israel at the Red Sea for His glory.

"Yet he saved them for his name's sake, that he might make known his mighty power" (Psalm 106:8).

Salvation for the glory of God.

"Help us, O God of our salvation, for the glory of your name; deliver us, and atone for our sins, for your name's sake!" (Psalm 79:9)

God predestined us for His glory.

"He predestined us for adoption to himself as sons through Jesus Christ, according to the purpose of his will, to the praise of his glorious grace, with which he has blessed us in the Beloved" (Ephesians 1:5, 6).

Christ's purpose in dying was to glorify God.
"Now is my soul troubled. And what shall I say? 'Father, save me from this hour'? But for this purpose I have come to this hour. Father, glorify your name" (John 12:27, 28).

Judgment of the wicked is for His glory.
"But for this purpose I have raised you up, to show you my power, so that my name may be proclaimed in all the earth" (Exodus 9:16).

He will return for His glory.
" . . . when he comes on that day to be glorified in his saints, and to be marveled at among all who have believed" (2 Thessalonians 1:10).

God is the most God-centered being in the universe. Everything He does is to reveal more of who He is so that He will receive maximum glory.

He is also *worthy* of worship. "Worthy are you, our Lord and God, to receive glory and honor and power, for you created all things, and by your will they existed and were created" (Revelation 4:11). God is central, not man. "For from him and through him and to him are all things. To him be glory forever" (Romans 11:36).

Indeed, we are told to do everything for His glory: "Whether then you eat or drink or whatever you do, do all for the glory of God" (1 Corinthians 10:31). If it is holy and righteous for us to do everything for His glory, cannot the same be said of God? In fact, if we do not do something for God's glory, it is idolatry.

The same is true of God. If God acts for a reason other than His glory, He would be guilty of idolatry. Acting for something else would place it as a more worthy goal than Himself. God is never guilty of idolatry; He always places the greatest value on that which is infinitely valuable: Himself.

God's glory is infinitely more valuable than me. This is the ultimate reason behind everything He does. The Bible mentions other goals, but they are *secondary* goals that are a means to glorify Himself. God's glory is the *ultimate* goal, not the salvation of man. The salvation of people is part of God's goal, but it is a secondary goal, not the ultimate one.

Let me illustrate the difference between ultimate and secondary goals. If you plan to drive from New York City to Orlando, your ultimate goal would be Orlando. However, to reach that city, you must pass through many cities before arriving (Philadelphia, Baltimore, Washington D.C., etc.). These cities are secondary goals because they are necessary to achieve the ultimate goal, arriving in Orlando. They are goals, but they are valuable, mostly, because of their relationship to the ultimate goal. In the same way, God's ultimate goal is His glory. One of His key secondary goals is man's salvation.

How did this knowledge change me? It changed my view of worship, love, and serving God.

It turned my worship upside down. I saw more of the greatness and worth of God. The universe does not revolve around me; it is all about glorifying God. I exist for God.

It is important to remember that when we glorify God we do not add to God's glory. We simply put His glory on display. We help others see it more clearly. Just as holding a telescope to someone's eye helps them see the stars more clearly, when we glorify God we help others see Him more clearly. John Piper explains:

> It may get a dangerous twist if we are not careful. *Glorify* is like the word beautify. But beautify usually means "make something more beautiful than it is," improve its beauty. That is emphatically not what we mean by *glorify* in relation to God. God cannot be made more glorious or more

beautiful than he is. He cannot be improved, "nor is he served by human hands, as though he needed anything" (Acts 17:25). *Glorify* does not mean adding more glory to God.[6]

God is perfect. If I could add to God's glory, He would be less than perfect and not fully God. Also, God does not need me. If God needed me to add to His glory then He would not be complete in Himself. He would be dependent on His creature. Glorifying God follows this path: recognizing His glory, submitting to His glory, being satisfied in His glory, then showing and telling others of His glory.

Rather than treating worship as something I do to add to God's glory or something I do for God, I must view it as delight. Worship is when I delight in God's glory and put it on display!

To live for His glory alone is to align with God. It is how we travel with the current.

It is important to God that we align with His goal of glorifying Himself because He wants His creation to joyfully declare His praise.

THE BIG PICTURE

If my desire is to be pleasing and useful to God, and God's desire is to glorify Himself, how should that affect my life and ministry?

It means everything I do should be done to glorify God and point others to His greatness.

That is my purpose.

But understanding that I should live for God's glory is one thing; knowing how to do this is another.

Serving God in a way that is useful and pleasing to Him is about aligning every part of my life to His desire. Namely, living in a way that glorifies God in the greatest possible way.

How does this help us know how to become the kind of servant God looks to? Here's how:

God is looking for servants who will glorify His name in all they do. He wants to display His glory in the greatest possible way; therefore He is looking for servants who best display His glory and won't get in the way of His glory being seen. This is the lens through which God looks at His servants to determine if they are useful. This is how He chooses whether He will give His strong support.

The rest of the book seeks to answer this question:
What kind of servant most glorifies God?

Discovering the answer won't make you perfect. But it will help you grow. For me, discovering the answer has helped me evaluate, daily, how to grow and change to become the servant God wants me to be. We will always be in need of growth on this side of Heaven, but seeing our life through God's lens helps us prioritize how we live and minister.

To answer this question we will consider practical ways to travel with the current of God's desire to glorify Himself: Connecting to the Spring, Removing the Barriers, and Connecting to Others.

Knowing the answers is only the first step. Your heart must also be changed.

If God reveals areas of your life which are hindering His glory from being seen, are you willing to change?

Are you committed to traveling with God's current by living for His glory?

If you are, let's dive deeper into the heart.

Part 2:

THE STREAM – CONNECTING TO THE SPRING

A few years ago I faced a trial that took the wind out of my sails and left me feeling defeated and discouraged. My natural tendency when problems arise is to try to work more, to push and push until the problem goes away.

This time I didn't. I remember realizing: I don't actually need to do more right now. I need more of God! So I stopped working on the problem and took some extra time with God that day to simply be still before Him. Not to fix the problem, but to simply spend time with my Creator.

As I was still, God used some ants to show me more about Himself. Yes, ants. I saw the ants building a nest in the grass, and God reminded me that just as He provides for the sparrow, He provides for the ants. Day in and day out since the beginning of the world, everything is under His power and control. Even the ants.

Do you know what my response was as God reminded me of His greatness? Worship. My heart worshiped God for His greatness. I realized I had no reason to worry. All my problems were under His control. But I needed to be still to remember this. I needed to stop trying to fix my problems so I could hear His still, small voice. I needed to "be still, and know that [God is] God" (Psalm 46:10).

What did my soul find? It found joy, confident faith, and peace for my soul. My soul found strength!

Had the situation changed? Not at all. Nothing had changed— and yet everything had. Not only had my perspective changed, my power had also changed. I moved from feeling defeated to having confidence in God's power to bring about His plan.

In that strength, I was able to face the situation before me.

Jesus said, "Apart from me you can do nothing" (John 15:5). God is the spring. Without God we are a dry streambed. When we are connected to God, we become a flowing stream.

Chapter 4

THE STREAM

Am I lost in awe, or have I lost my awe?

"But they who wait for the Lord shall renew their strength"
(ISAIAH 40:31).

WHAT IS THE STREAM?

We are like an empty stream, yet one perfectly designed to channel water to far-off places. The stream is not the source; the stream is only the conduit for delivery.

Only when God's power fills us can we minister in a way that brings about true spiritual change. We must stay connected to the source, the spring and fountain of life. As soon as we are cut off from the source of water, we run dry.

How do we stay connected to the spring?

Worship. Our heart stays filled with God when we stay connected to Him through worship. Unlike other activities, worship fills our soul with joy in God. This joy spills over to others in ministry.

WHY DOES WORSHIP MATTER TO US?

1. Without worship, your ministry is worthless.

Worship matters because it is possible to serve in a way that doesn't please God!

It's easy to become like the Pharisees who "honor me with their lips, but their heart is far from me; in vain do they worship me, teaching as doctrines the commandments of men" (Matthew 15:8, 9). Even if we serve with great zeal and energy, we may not be pleasing to God.

Outward actions only honor God when they come from a worshipful heart. The state of your heart is essential because actions flow from your heart. "Keep your heart with all vigilance, for from it flow the springs of life" (Proverbs 4:23).

One person can preach from a humble heart and that action be clearly displayed as worship. Another person can preach the same message from a proud heart that loves to be "seen by men"; this is not worship. The action does not determine if something is worship. The heart does. The heart either purifies or defiles an action.

God is not simply looking at your actions, He is looking for actions that flow from a heart of worship.

"The heart is deceitful above all things, and desperately sick; who can understand it? 'I the Lord search the heart and test the mind,* to give every man according to his ways, according to the fruit of his deeds'" (Jeremiah 17:9, 10).

"For the eyes of the LORD run to and fro throughout the whole earth, to give strong support to those whose heart is blameless toward him" (2 Chronicles 16:9).

It is vital to know if you are serving the Lord in a way that pleases Him.

A proper understanding of the God we worship and serve is foundational to service. This understanding leads to worship and worship leads to service. Therefore, everything stands or falls on worship. Without worship as the foundation and center of your life, your service will fail. Service starts with worship.

Worship matters to you because without it you will be serving in vain.

2. Without worship, you dry up.

Missionaries, pastors, and others in ministry are usually very hard workers. But it's also easy in ministry to begin slowly depending on our strength. Eventually, this leads to burnout because we are carrying burdens we're not meant to carry. Maybe we never reach the point of burnout, but if we focus on problems and trials our souls become weary. We become like Peter, who took his eyes off the Lord and began to focus on the waves. When this happens we begin to sink.

Like an empty streambed, we must replenish our soul daily through worship and rely on God for strength.

In ministry, you need strength to face the trials that inevitably will come. These trials are like the sun that evaporates the water from the stream. The more intense the trial, the faster your strength evaporates. Not only do you need strength to endure, you also need to have something to share with others.

You cannot minister from an empty cup! You minister from the overflow of your life.

WHY DOES WORSHIP MATTER TO GOD?

Imagine a servant who works hard out of duty to the king, but not out of joy. The servant tells others to worship the king because of his greatness, but the servant himself never takes time to worship.

Would this servant honor the king? No. The servant makes the king look like a terrible taskmaster. Serving merely out of duty and not joyful worship does not make God look great or satisfying.

Great kings are worshiped.

A worshiping servant exalts the king because he himself is in awe of the king's greatness. He serves with joy because he is calling others to join him in worship, not merely fulfill his duty. Because God's goal is His glory, He will use worshiping servants.

1. Worship matters because it fuels the messenger and validates the message.

Worship is before work. Stillness is before service. I am a worshiper first and a worker second. The reason worship should precede work is because worship fuels work. Worship sets the worker ablaze so he or she may burn with passion for God and the world.

To delight in His glory we must sit at the Savior's feet. We need firsthand knowledge of the glory of God. Having tasted and seen it for ourselves, we can then share our personal delight with others. "Oh, taste and see that the Lord is good!" (Psalm 34:8)

How can we declare, "Come, behold the works of the Lord" (Psalm 46:8) if we have not beheld them ourselves?

How can we say "delight yourself in the Lord" (Psalm 37:4) if we do not delight ourselves in the Lord?

We need to be affected by God so we can give personal testimony to the goodness, greatness, and grace of God. For God to receive glory, others must see gladhearted worshipers.

Our actions are important in serving God, but our tendency is to neglect the more important things. We neglect worship. We become like Martha and focus on service.

If your heart is unaffected by the Most High God, how can you expect your listeners to be affected?

2. Worship matters because it fulfills God's goal: His glory.

What happens if we reverse the order? If we are workers first and worshipers second, then we treat God as deficient and ourselves as sufficient.

The goal of service and ministry is to show the glory and greatness of God, not to help God out as if He needs us.

God does not need our help. We are the ones who need His help.

We do not serve God because He is needy.
"The God who made the world and everything in it, being Lord of heaven and earth, does not live in temples made by man, nor is he served by human hands, as though he needed anything, since he himself gives to all mankind life and breath and everything" (Acts 17:24, 25).

We have nothing to offer God that He did not give us.
"What do you have that you did not receive? If then you received it, why do you boast as if you did not receive it?" (1 Corinthians 4:7)

If we treat God as needy, it makes God look small because we appear to be helping God. The goal in service is to glorify God. If we serve God as if He is needy, we do not glorify Him! Instead, we make ourselves look big and powerful while making God look small and helpless.

Because of this, God wants worshipers who work, not workers who worship. There is a vast difference between the two.

God wants worshipers who set Him as first place in their hearts and lives, and then He uses them to proclaim His greatness before others. If we are not worshipers first and have not first exalted Him to the highest place in our hearts, we will be poor examples of exalting Him before others.

Lives that are changed by worship will honor God more than lives that simply seek to do something for God.

We cannot proclaim well publicly what we do not proclaim well privately. We cannot glorify Him in our actions if our heart does not worship Him.

The world needs to see that we are servants of the all-powerful, most satisfying God—not a needy God. They need to see that God is worthy of our worship, not just worthy of our work.

HOW DO WE CONNECT WITH GOD IN WORSHIP?

This is essential for all of life and ministry because it connects us to our source of power. This is what fills our stream with the life-giving water of God.

The starting point for worship is this: *waiting upon the Lord.*

"The Lord is the everlasting God, the Creator of the ends of the earth. He does not faint or grow weary; his understanding is unsearchable. He gives power to the faint, and to him who has no might he increases strength. Even youths shall faint and be weary, and young men shall fall exhausted; but they who wait for the Lord shall renew their strength; they shall mount up with wings like eagles; they shall run and not be weary; they shall walk and not faint" (Isaiah 40:28-31).

So what does it mean to wait upon the Lord?

From these verses, there are four parts to consider: being still, satisfaction, owning our weaknesses, and confident prayer.

1. Being Still

" . . . they who wait for the Lord" (Isaiah 40:31).

Stillness in work: Am I putting the Master before the ministry?

Being still is ceasing from our labor, or delaying it. Elsewhere we are reminded that "in quietness and in trust shall be your strength" (Isaiah 30:15). The psalmist tells us to "be still, and know that I am God" (Psalm 46:10). The NASB translation of this verse says "cease striving."

It is easy to rush in ministry. When we have our "quiet time," do we actually quiet our heart? Do we leave enough time to "be still," or is our mind still thinking about what we need to do?

Our default is to *do*, not to *be still*. We try to find our strength in activity and busyness, but that is not where it is found. Rather, our strength is found in quietness, stillness, and waiting on the Lord.

Being still is an act of faith.

In life there are things that have to be done, but are we taking time to be still? For me, when I face tasks or problems, I am tempted to do more. When this happens, I forget something: the true work is done by God, not me. When I stop working to spend time in worship and prayer, it's an act of faith because I must trust God to work in ways I cannot. I am ceasing from my striving.

I used to feel guilty about taking more time to pray because I somehow felt lazy or that I wasn't being busy enough. Then God reminded me of the example of Jesus. Even though He only had three years to minister and endless needs to meet, he still took a great deal of time for stillness.

If Jesus took time for stillness, I can follow His example.

"And when it was day, he departed and went into a desolate place" (Luke 4:42).

"But he would withdraw to desolate places and pray" (Luke 5:16).

Stillness must come before service, and worship before work. Are you taking time to be still?

Not only do we need to be still in our work, we also need stillness in body, mind, and heart.

Stillness in body: Am I taking time for rest and replenishment?

My body needs stillness. I am constantly self-experimenting to find what helps my body handle stress. There are times I may have mentally overcome some stressful problem, but my body may still be distressed—or even depressed. Figuring out what replenishes and energizes me physically helps me prioritize key activities in my schedule. (For me, these include: daily devotions, regular exercise, stretching, enough sleep, eating healthy, regular vacations, sabbath rest, internet/email breaks, fun activities, watching comedies, reading, solitude, enjoying nature, and more.)

I minister in body and soul. If my body burns out, I have nothing left to give. If I take time for regular replenishment, I will endure longer. (For more on this topic, check out the Appendix "Overflowing Health.")

When I won't slow down for rest and replenishment, it's often an indication of pride. Pride makes me think that my part of the work is so valuable that the ministry would cease if I chose to rest. But God doesn't need me to accomplish His work. That's why God commanded Israel to keep the Sabbath: He wanted them to trust His work, not their work.

Stillness in mind: Am I following God one step at a time?

I also need to be still in mind. It can be easy to be still in body but have my mind thinking about all I need to do. I may not be physically moving, but my mind is still carrying the burden. My mind is not at rest.

One of my tendencies when facing a problem is to try to figure out all the next steps. I want to figure out steps one through thirty-seven. Like one of those "choose your own adventure" books, I run different scenarios in my mind until I think I have the right steps to get to the desired end. But when I do this I am trusting myself to fix the problem. If I am worrying about it, I am carrying it. If I am resting, I have relinquished control.

Recently, God challenged me to face problems differently. Instead of trying to think through every step to fix a problem, I ask just one question: What's my *next* step? This clarifies what my responsibility is and what God's responsibility is. Often after taking my next step, God works in a way I never would have planned, and He fixes the problem. Sometimes when I take the time to be still, I come back to my work to find He has already resolved the problem! If I try to figure out every step, I can become paralyzed in indecision and fear. Taking one step at a time relieves incredible stress because I am not carrying the burden God is meant to carry.

One litmus test for me is sleep. Do I wake up thinking about solutions to problems? These verses always challenge me: "Unless the Lord builds the house, those who build it labor in vain. Unless the Lord watches over the city, the watchman stays awake in vain. It is in vain that you rise up early and go late to rest, eating the bread of anxious toil; for *he gives to his beloved sleep*" (Psalm 127:1, 2). Sleep is a gift from God; it's also an act of faith to receive. Letting my mind be still in sleep demonstrates that I am relinquishing control over a problem because I trust that the God who needs no sleep is still at work. It's completely giving something to God, and not trying to take it back to micromanage the outcome. It is my heart saying, in faith: "God's got this."

Stillness in heart: Is my heart at peace?

I need to be still in heart. Why is God always at peace? Because He is never frustrated. His plan always succeeds! God says: "I will be exalted among the nations, I will be exalted in the earth!" (Psalm 46:10) That is an absolute promise. God is far more committed to His glory and His plan than I am.

Why is my heart not always at peace? Because things don't always go according to my plan. I want my plan and God's plan to both be about Him getting the glory. But here is the problem:

my plan usually involves Kyle's comfort, while God's plan doesn't always include this.

I must continually remind my heart that God's ultimate goal is His glory. When God allows problems, His plan is still accomplished. Problems affect my comfort, not God's plan. If I love God's glory more than my comfort, then I will be able to look at troubles and weaknesses through this lens: they are being used by God to highlight His glory.

Not only am I never outside of God's plan, I am also never outside of His presence. "The Lord of hosts is with us" (Psalm 46:11). He promises to "never leave us" (Hebrews 13:5). No matter how big the storm or problem in life, God is bigger, and He will carry me through.

Paul says to "let the peace of Christ rule in your hearts" (Colossians 3:15). If worry is ruling our hearts, then Christ is not. When Christ's peace is ruling, it is because He is on the throne. Every problem is under His control. He is Lord of the storm and the sea, so we need not worry.

When we allow the peace of Christ to rule in our hearts, we can face life and ministry with unwavering confidence.

Are you taking the time to be still?

2. Satisfaction

" . . . they who wait for the Lord" (Isaiah 40:31).

Why do we wait?

Our waiting is *for* the Lord. We seek Him because He alone both saves and satisfies our soul. The deep longing of our heart is to know Him more and more. Even compared to all that this world has to offer, we can "count everything as loss because of the surpassing worth of knowing Christ Jesus my Lord" (Philippians 3:8). Like David, we can say that we "have no good apart from you" (Psalm 16:2).

Worship erupts when our heart beholds its treasure.

"The Lord is the everlasting God, the Creator of the ends of the earth. He does not faint or grow weary; his understanding is unsearchable" (Isaiah 40:28).

Worship is stopping to say "Wow!"

How often do we simply stop to be with the Lord? To sit and be lost in awe at who He is? In delaying or ceasing from our labor to be alone with God, we are demonstrating through our actions that we love the Master more than the ministry. We are saying through our actions: "Lord, I want more of you! You are my treasure!"

The story of Martha and Mary shows a common mistake in serving God. It also shows the starting point for service. God intends that we start by waiting in worship.

"Now as they went on their way, Jesus entered a village. And a woman named Martha welcomed him into her house. And she had a sister called Mary, who sat at the Lord's feet and listened to his teaching. But Martha was distracted with much serving. And she went up to him and said, 'Lord, do you not care that my sister has left me to serve alone? Tell her then to help me.' But the Lord answered her, 'Martha, Martha, you are anxious and troubled about many things, but one thing is necessary. Mary has chosen the good portion, which will not be taken away from her'" (Luke 10:38-42).

Mary sat, listening, with her attention focused on the Lord; Martha was busy and "distracted with much serving." When we are distracted, our focus moves from where it should be to where it should not be. Martha was focused on serving; Mary was focused on the Lord.

Jesus didn't say that serving is wrong. The Bible tells us we are to serve. Paul "worked harder than any of them" (1 Corinthians 15:10). We are to serve others and the Lord. Martha's focus was wrong. Her focus was on *service*, not the *Lord*. In other words, she was more concerned about what she was doing rather than who she was serving.

Many of us make the same mistake. We want to serve God and bring Him glory, so we *do*. It is not wrong to do things. But worship should always precede work.

God alone satisfies our souls. When our soul is satisfied in Him it finds the daily strength to serve. The service comes out of an overflow of our hearts. We must take time to worship before serving!

What happens far too often? We mentally understand the truth that God is above all, but we don't meditate long enough to become lost in wonder. We must ask ourselves: Am I lost in awe, or have I lost my awe?

Worship is always a response to greatness we have seen. When we see something we consider great, worship is the response of the heart.

What happens when we see a great sports play? We respond by saying: "Wow! That was awesome!" When you stand at the base of the mountains and see their majestic peaks, you say: "Wow! That is awesome! What a Creator!" That is worship. You give credit to the One who acted out the greatness.

All around us is greatness and beauty. Creation displays the glory of God. In God's Word He has revealed Himself so we can understand more of His greatness and glorify Him.

True worship is a place of self-forgetfulness as we stand amazed at God. It's all about Him, not us.

To become a worshiper of God, we need to see His greatness. Like Mary, we need to take time to see God's revelation of

Himself. Like Moses, our daily prayer should be: "Please show me your glory" (Exodus 33:18). His glory is our heart's treasure!

Why is worship the first step to service? To call others to worship God, we must first worship Him. Our hearts must worship Him above all else. Otherwise, we are calling others to worship someone we ourselves do not truly worship! If we do this, we will be trying to serve others from an empty stream.

If you want to serve others and change lives from an overflowing stream, your personal worship of God and satisfaction in Him should be your number one priority. He alone can fill you to overflowing!

May our hearts cry out with David:

"O God, you are my God; earnestly I seek you; my soul thirsts for you; my flesh faints for you, as in a dry and weary land where there is no water. So I have looked upon you in the sanctuary, beholding your power and glory. Because your steadfast love is better than life, my lips will praise you. So I will bless you as long as I live; in your name I will lift up my hands. My soul will be satisfied as with fat and rich food, and my mouth will praise you with joyful lips" (Psalm 63:1-5).

David *sought God*. David *beheld* God's glory. David *praised* God. David was *satisfied* with God. If our heart is truly worshiping God, these actions will be evident. But if we fail to seek and behold the greatness of God, we will never be lost in awe. Our stream will run dry.

Are you lost in awe, or have you lost your awe?

3. Owning Our Weakness

"He gives power to the faint, and to him who has no might he increases strength" (Isaiah 40:29).

Owning our weakness connects us to God's strength. When we are weak, then we are strong! God uses weakness to highlight His strength and sufficiency.

What reveals our weakness? Trials. God uses trials to put our weakness on display.

How many battles did the Israelites fight that were in their favor? None! If their odds of winning looked favorable, God would often remove their advantage so His power would be clearly seen!

God is still God. God is still making victory impossible apart from Him.

When God allows us to step into a trial, He may be getting ready to work for His glory. Historically, this is how God prefers to work. Remember Gideon? He started off with an army one-fifth the size of the Midianites—and then God made the odds even worse!

"The Lord said to Gideon, 'The people with you are too many for me to give the Midianites into their hand, lest Israel boast over me, saying, "My own hand has saved me"'" (Judges 7:2).

God uses trials to show that He alone deserves the credit. Trials make it clear to the world that we are not in control. Everyone can see we don't have the ability or strength to overcome the problem. Therefore, when God works, He gets the glory, not us.

Our lives are like Gideon's army. He is going to stack the odds against us so that our dependence is completely on Him, and He gets *all* the glory.

This is why Paul could rejoice in troubles and trials. The credit would go to God, not Paul.

"But he said to me, 'My grace is sufficient for you, for my power is made perfect in weakness.' Therefore I will boast all the more gladly of my weaknesses, so that the power of Christ may rest upon me. For the sake of Christ, then, I am content with weaknesses, insults, hardships, persecutions, and calamities. For when I am weak, then I am strong" (2 Corinthians 12:9, 10).

When God allows trials and troubles to come, He is wanting us to turn to Him, not quit. God usually allows problems to increase to highlight our weaknesses before He does something great. He may cause our strategies to fail—which is why the best strategies are those that highlight our weaknesses and His strength.

Trials remind me of my weaknesses. They use a lot of time and energy, but they don't slow God's plan. When a new trial comes, God reminds me to "be still and know that I am God. I will be exalted among the nations, I will be exalted in the earth!" (Psalm 46:10)

Success does not depend on me; it depends on the mighty power of God to do the impossible. The God who made the heavens and holds everything in the palm of His hands is never worried or concerned. His eternal plan is still marching on. The "totally unexpected" events that happen are totally planned by God.

Hard circumstances do not stop God's plan or the spread of the gospel. They are Satan's tactics to discourage me. But where does my hope come from? Does my joy and hope come from my comfort and lack of problems, or are they rooted in the fact that God is at work? His supernatural power is not deterred or slowed. His plan is not stopped. Yes, I will have problems as I go, but my joy must be in the promises of God and the confidence that He is still at work. Problems affect my comfort, but they do not affect the outcome.

We must learn to embrace weakness. God loves to highlight His strength by reminding us of our utter weakness. Remember Joseph in prison, Joshua against the Philistines, Gideon against the Midianites, Daniel in the lion's den, and Paul's many trials.

God also wants us to guard against self-reliance. He commanded Israel to not multiply chariots or horses so they would trust in His strength, not their strength.

Weakness has been one of God's primary tools through the centuries. It is never comfortable, but I don't expect God to change His strategy anytime soon.

Owning our weakness is essential if we are to stay aligned with God's ultimate goal of bringing glory to Himself. When God allows weakness and trials, we must remember He is at work.

Are you owning your weakness so God's power can be seen?

4. Confident Prayer (in Faith)

" . . . they who wait for the Lord" (Isaiah 40:31).

Confident prayer is not explicit here in Isaiah 40, but it is implied in the waiting.

Another passage illustrates this well: "I waited patiently for the LORD; he inclined to me and heard my cry" (Psalm 40:1).

I ask for God's help, then I wait patiently for Him to respond.

When I cease from my labor I am saying by my non-action that He alone is able to accomplish the task. I am not depending on my labor alone, I am trusting in faith that God is going to work. I am saying, "Lord, I need more of you!"

God loves to answer this kind of prayer because this means He gets all the glory.

One of my favorite verses is Psalm 46:10, which we have highlighted a few times. Still, it's worth meditating on once more at this point: "Be still, and know that I am God. I will be exalted among the nations, I will be exalted in the earth!"

This verse reminds me to be still, to worship, to be weak, and to trust. Trust is faith that He will be exalted. He promises to work for His glory. If my plans to glorify God aren't going as planned, then maybe—just maybe—God has a different (better!) plan to glorify Himself.

Do you realize God is never worried? That's because He knows His plan is going to be accomplished. When things aren't going right, take heart; they are going the way God planned them! They are going to work out for His maximum glory. I don't have to understand the plan, but I can trust and have faith that God's plan is best.

When you pray, is your heart confident in God's plan?

THE BIG PICTURE

Why is worship essential to serving God? Service flows from a worshiping heart. As we wait on the Lord in worship, we connect ourselves to the spring, our source of life and power. We have no strength apart from God. If we stay connected to God in worship, we will be like a stream that never runs dry!

God desires to put His glory on display for all to see. One of the ways He does this is by showing that all the power comes from Him and not ourselves. Another way He does this is by showing He is more satisfying to us than our ministry or anything else this world has to offer. He is our treasure. This puts God's beauty on display. God loves to use servants that make Him look great because He is worthy of all the glory.

If we are called to make wholehearted worshipers and disciples of Christ, then we must first be a wholehearted worshiper and disciple. We must model the message.

"Oh come, let us worship and bow down; let us kneel before the Lord, our Maker! For he is our God, and we are the people of his pasture, and the sheep of his hand" (Psalm 95:6, 7).

Worship is the wellspring of service. Without worship, service fails.

Part 3:

THE BARRIERS - REMOVING THE BARRIERS

Laying under our vehicle in South Africa, I was struggling to remove the oil filter. I could feel frustration building to the point of getting angry. (Which is always a brilliant idea: to get upset at an inanimate object.) But the annoyance went deeper than simple irritation with an oil filter. The greater frustration was that I felt everything was going wrong and preventing me from "ministry." I was not able to do the important, *spiritual* part of my life.

Because of this frustration, I let myself get upset, angry, and impatient.

But then God convicted me. I realized the way I was dealing with this anger and frustration was a reflection of what was in my heart. It revealed a few things about my heart:

- I was obviously not walking in the Spirit because I was not demonstrating one of the fruits of the Spirit: patience.

- I was allowing my circumstances, rather than truth from God's Word, to determine my reactions.

- I was taking greater joy in not having problems (comfort) than I was in God.

- Even though I said I believed in God's sovereignty, I still didn't always love it or submit to it. Because when problems came, I would get upset rather than trusting that God allowed the problem. Getting mad is like shaking my fist at God and saying, "*My* way would have been better than your way!"

That day God challenged me with something that so deeply impacted my life it has affected every day since. It literally flipped the order of importance in my life.

My greater focus up to that point was on serving God. I definitely pursued knowing and obeying God, but it felt like multiple pursuits. Serving God and my relationship with God felt like different things I needed to do to please God. Sadly, my love of the ministry and serving was often greater than my *love of the Master*.

Here was the truth God challenged my heart with:

Kyle, who you are is more important than what you do because what you do flows out of who you are.

This thought absolutely flipped my view of serving God on its head. God doesn't just want my actions; He also wants my heart. He wants all of me. My actions flow from my heart and show my heart.

Again, remember this vital verse: "Keep your heart with all vigilance, for from it flow the springs of life" (Proverbs 4:23).

Above everything else, I must become the kind of person God has called me to be. Every moment of every day, my relationship with God is the single most important part of my life. Without the heart, ministry fails.

The reason is simple: if I am called to make wholehearted worshipers and disciples of Christ, then I must first be a wholehearted worshiper and disciple. I must model the message. As I do, the Holy Spirit works through me with His power to create spiritual fruit. Does God promise spiritual fruit to those with the best planning strategy or the most activity? No! He promises "strong support" to those whose hearts are fully his (2 Chronicles 16:9) and spiritual fruit to "whoever abides in [Him]" (John 15:4, 5). Even more amazing, He is searching for such hearts!

Becoming a servant who is pleasing and useful to God is not out of reach; it is attainable. It starts with your heart.

Everything is an overflow of the heart. Who you are is more important than what you do, because what you do flows out of who you are. What kind of heart are your actions overflowing from?

If ministry is an overflow of the heart, the next critical question becomes: *Are you allowing sin to remain in your life that creates barriers in your relationship with God?*

If we have barriers that are hindering our relationship with God, we won't be effective in ministry. Barriers restrict the flow of God's power through us.

Chapter 5

HEART BARRIERS

*Am I allowing sin to remain in my life that creates
barriers in my relationship with God?*

*"For the eyes of the LORD run to and fro throughout the whole
earth, to give strong support to those whose heart is blameless
toward him"* (2 CHRONICLES 16:9).

WHAT ARE BARRIERS?

Barriers are anything that hinders water flowing through a stream. If a stream has boulders, gravel, or trash, it is going to block the mouth of the stream and dam up water. The barriers only allow a trickle of water downstream.

Only the life-giving water that gets past the barriers will reach others. In other words, if God's power doesn't flow through us unhindered, our ministry is merely an overflow of our own effort. If only a trickle of God's power gets past the barriers in our life, then our ministry will only have . . . a trickle of God's power.

I don't know about you, but I want more than a trickle of God's power flowing through me; I want a flood.

My passion is that each of us would grow to be more effective in our ministry to others. I want each of us to serve God in a way that we bear much fruit in our lives.

God's Word reminds us that "apart from me you can do nothing" (John 15:5). It also reminds us His strength is "able to do far more abundantly than all we ask or think, according to the power at work within us" (Ephesians 3:20). God's power can accomplish more through us than we can imagine!

I trust the same is true of you as it is of me:

- You want to be used by God for His glory.

- You don't want a wasted life.

- You want God's power to flow in and through you to make a name for Himself.

Removing barriers is absolutely essential if you desire to be used by God.

Think back to Chapter 1, "God's Heart Search." Why does God choose to use some people in mighty ways and others not so much? He chose to use some of His children in greater ways (Noah, Moses, David, Isaiah, Joseph, and Daniel among them). Was there something that set them apart?

We know the power comes from God, but what is *our* role in being used by Him?

Do we have a part, or are we completely out of the equation?

I believe we have a part in the equation, but it is not something that we add to the equation—it is something that is *removed*. God doesn't look at us and say: "Wow, I hope they join my team. They have so much potential!"

It doesn't work that way.

When God uses someone, He goes *with* them. His power works through them. This means if we desire to be used by God, He needs to be *with* us. Consider these words spoken to King Asa: "The LORD is with you while you are with him" (2 Chronicles 15:2). God going with us is contingent on us being with God, our heart being fully His.

We're like an empty stream. We have nothing to offer. But when the barriers that hinder God's life-giving water and power are removed, we are filled and become life-giving streams to others.

How can the barriers and hindrances be removed to allow the spring to flow freely through us?

At one point in my life, I was taught that the way to battle sin was to "let go and let God." The reasoning was that we don't have the power to fight and therefore just need to surrender to Him. While there is truth in this, it is only a partial truth. The result of this half-truth is defeatism. It is like sitting down on the battlefield and saying "God, I don't have the strength, please conquer this sin!"

In Scripture we see another truth that complements our weakness. It is that we fight in the strength that God supplies. Paul highlights these complementary truths when he tells us to "work out your own salvation with fear and trembling" and then immediately follows by saying: "for it is God who works in you, both to will and to work for his good pleasure" (Philippians 2:12, 13). We do play a part, but it is not in our strength, it's in His strength. We are working because God is working.

In his book *The Pursuit of Holiness*, Jerry Bridges writes:

"To put to death the misdeeds of the body, then, is to destroy the strength and vitality of sin as it tries to reign in our bodies.

It must be clear to us that mortification, though it is something we do, cannot be carried out in our own strength. Well did the Puritan John Owen say, 'Mortification from a self-strength, carried on by ways of self-invention, unto the end of a self-righteousness is the soul and substance of all false religion.' Mortification must be done by the strength and under the direction of the Holy Spirit.

Owen says further, 'The Spirit alone is sufficient for this work. All ways and means without Him are useless. He is the great efficient. He is the One who gives life and strength to our efforts.'

But though mortification must be done by the strength and under the direction of the Holy Spirit, it is nevertheless a work which we must do. Without the Holy Spirit's strength there will be no mortification, but without our working in His strength there will also be not mortification."[7]

As we go through the next few chapters on heart barriers and battling sin, remember these complementary truths. At times I will highlight one of the truths, but the goal is not to neglect the other truth. Both must always be present. View these chapters through this lens.

Moving forward with this lens, let's look again at 2 Chronicles 16:9 from the perspective of barriers.

"For the eyes of the LORD run to and fro throughout the whole earth, to give strong support to those whose heart is blameless toward him" (2 Chronicles 16:9).

What role do barriers play in God's power flowing through us?

1. Like water, God is conducting a search.

Consider a spring of water. The spring has an endless supply. Whenever there is a stream connected to the spring, water instantly flows. If there are barriers, the water is dammed up and pools. When water is restricted and dammed up, it is nevertheless continually searching for an opportunity to flow—always.

What is water looking for? No resistance. No barriers. No hindrances. When it finds no resistance, it flows and fills any stream.

In the same way, God is searching for streams to flow through. We don't have any power in and of ourselves, but we are part of the equation. God is searching just as water searches. He is searching for hearts without barriers.

2. Like water, God pours out His power on those He finds.

" . . . to give strong support . . . " (2 Chronicles 16:9)

Not only is water always searching, it also has incredible power. In 2019 a dam broke near Midland, Michigan, releasing a flood of water on the town. The instant the barrier was removed, the water flowed. The water didn't hesitate—it flowed with power. In this case, the flood was a bad thing. But as we consider the power of God flowing through us to others, it's a good thing.

When water has barriers, it moves only in a trickle. When water is unhindered, it flows in a flood.

The barriers in our life directly affect how God's power flows through us. We don't add to God's power, but if we allow sin to remain it limits how much He fills and overflows from us.

3. Like water, God's power flows to those whose heart is completely His.

" . . . to those whose heart is blameless [or whole] toward him" (2 Chronicles 16:9, ESV).

" . . . those whose heart is completely His" (2 Chronicles 16:9, NASB).

God is looking for hearts that are fully open to Him, hearts with no barriers. When He finds such hearts He can flow unhindered through them.

God doesn't want hearts that are mostly His. He wants hearts that are *completely* His. He wants hearts that are whole toward Him.

He wants all of our heart, not just part of it.

We must allow Christ to completely fill our heart if we desire Him to overflow in our actions. For Christ to overflow from us, He must fill our being. In the physical world, two things cannot occupy the same space. Water cannot occupy the same space as a rock. The same is true in the spiritual world. Two spiritual things cannot occupy the same space. The areas in our heart where sin dwells hinder God from completely filling us. Sin is filling the space where God should be. We cannot live wholeheartedly for God when God doesn't have our entire heart. To seek God with our whole heart is to seek more of His presence. To have more of His presence means He will fill the space sin once filled.

He only fills spaces unhindered by the barriers of sin.

If we submit fully to His power, He will push the barriers out of our life.

THE BARRIER

The barrier between us and God is sin.

What is sin?

Sin is the violation of God's holiness. While holiness is perfection, sin is when we fail to live according to God's perfect standard.

The rest of Part 3 of this book will look at three key manifestations of sin: *unbelief, disobedience,* and *pride.* I realize there is some overlap between these. For example, not believing God's promises (unbelief) is a root of disobedience, and pride is a form of disobedience.

So why focus on these three? There are two primary reasons.

The first reason God draws special attention to these three things is they hinder His glory from being seen in different ways. When unbelief, disobedience, and pride are removed, it allows others to see the fullness of God's glory.

The second reason is that God repeatedly says He desires the absence of these three. In other words, God is looking for the opposite.

God is looking for the barrier of *unbelief* to be removed so we can be filled with faith.

He is looking for the barrier of *disobedience* to be removed so we can be filled with holiness.

He is looking for the barrier of *pride* to be removed so we can be filled with humility.

God is looking for hearts that are filled with faith, holiness, and humility. These are the hearts He strongly supports!

Chapter 6

_____

THE BARRIER OF UNBELIEF: PART 1

Does my faith make God look great?

"Without faith it is impossible to please him" (HEBREWS 11:6).

WHAT IS UNBELIEF?

Unbelief is choosing not to trust God or believe His promises. It is the opposite of faith.

WHAT IS FAITH?

Faith is choosing to trust in God and believe His promises.

"Now faith is the assurance of things hoped for, the conviction of things not seen" (Hebrews 11:1).

Faith is the seed from which all other visible, outward branches of our life grow. Without the seed of faith, we will not bear the true fruit of a changed life.

WHY DOES FAITH MATTER TO US?

First a warning: God will bless the work of our hands according to *His* plans, not ours. We cannot assume that if we have faith God must use us! To believe this would be trusting and relying upon our faith rather than God's power. It would be treating faith as a work we do to earn God's favor. We never bend God's arm, but we can rely on Him in faith to do what is impossible with us.

1. Faith is necessary to please God.

"For by it [faith] the people of old received their commendation" (Hebrews 11:2).

"By faith Enoch was taken up so that he should not see death, and he was not found, because God had taken him. Now before he was taken he was commended as having pleased God. And without faith it is impossible to please him, for whoever would draw near to God must believe that he exists and that he rewards those who seek him" (Hebrews 11:5, 6).

If my goal is to please God, then I must live how He commands. I must evaluate if I am walking by faith in *every* area of my life, not just the major areas. It is easy to deceive myself into thinking I am walking by faith when I am not. If I don't walk by faith it's impossible to please God, no matter how hard I serve.

2. Faith is necessary for God to spiritually bless our lives and ministry.

God makes many promises to those who trust Him, but He makes no promises to those who trust in themselves or something other than God.

If I desire the power of God to rest on me and my ministry, I must trust Him to do the work. I must pursue ministry in faith. Whether I am planning or doing ministry, everything must be done in faith and prayer.

When we act in faith, God is seen as great. He gets the glory. Because of this, God loves to work through servants who trust Him in faith.

"Truly, truly, I say to you, whoever believes in me will also do the works that I do; and greater works than these will he do, because I am going to the Father. Whatever you ask in my name, this I will do, that the Father may be glorified in the Son. *If you ask me anything in my name, I will do it*" (John 14:12-14).

"For truly, I say to you, if you have faith like a grain of mustard seed, you will say to this mountain, 'Move from here to there,' and it will move, and *nothing will be impossible for you*" (Matthew 17:20, 21).

"The *prayer of a righteous person has great power as it is working*. Elijah was a man with a nature like ours, and he prayed fervently that it might not rain, and for three years and six months it did not rain on the earth. Then he prayed again, and heaven gave rain, and the earth bore its fruit" (James 5:16-18).

"*If any of you lacks wisdom, let him ask God, who gives generously to all without reproach, and it will be given him. But let him ask in faith, with no doubting,* for the one who doubts is like a wave of the sea that is driven and tossed by the wind. For that person must not suppose that he will receive anything from the Lord; he is a double-minded man, unstable in all his ways" (James 1:5-8).

Confident prayer grows from faith that God is our provider. Confident prayer is evidence of inner faith.

Do we desire to be used by God for His glory? Then faith is essential!

God is looking to use people who trust Him. Faith doesn't guarantee God will use us, but it makes us useful. Faith qualifies us to be used by God. Just as a person needs to do or be many things to qualify for a top-level sports team, faith qualifies us to be used by God on His team. Unbelief disqualifies us because we are not pleasing to God (Hebrews 11:6). Our faith today influences our usefulness tomorrow.

Prayer is one of the best indicators of faith. If our life and ministry are rooted in faith, we will prioritize prayer. Instead of creating plans and strategies and then seeking God's blessing, prayer is the strategy. In other words, when we walk by faith there is a gap between our actions and what we desire God to do. Our actions and strategy are not enough. We cannot complete the task. God and prayer fill that gap. God loves to use people who prioritize prayer because they position themselves to allow God to show His glory. In other words, our plans and strategy are designed to fail unless God's power shows up. We don't have the answers or ability; God alone does!

3. Faith enables us to accomplish an impossible mission.

If God doesn't do the work, I will fail.

I may be able to accomplish man-made results in my own strength, but they will not yield spiritual results. I may be able to finish my to-do list or clear my inbox, but I can do those things without seeing any spiritual fruit. Ministry that matters is ministry that changes lives. The work God gave us is seeking the lost, but only God can cause the spiritually blind to see. Only God can cause the spiritually dead to live. Only God can clean the barriers out of the stream. We have been called to an impossible mission, but we have not been left alone to accomplish it!

"'Then who can be saved?'" Jesus looked at them and said, *'With man it is impossible, but not with God. For all things are possible with God'"* (Mark 10:26, 27).

"Not by might, nor by power, but *by my Spirit,* says the Lord of hosts" (Zechariah 4:6).

"Not that we are sufficient in ourselves to claim anything as coming from us, but our *sufficiency is from God,* who has made us sufficient to be ministers of a new covenant, not of the letter but of the Spirit. . . . But we have this treasure in jars of clay, to show that the surpassing power belongs to God and not to us" (2 Corinthians 3:5, 6; 4:7).

"But he said to me, *'My grace is sufficient for you,* for my power is made perfect in weakness.' Therefore I will boast all the more gladly of my weaknesses, so that the power of Christ may rest upon me. For the sake of Christ, then, I am content with weaknesses, insults, hardships, persecutions, and calamities. For when I am weak, then I am strong" (2 Corinthians 12:9, 10).

"Abide in me, and I in you. *As the branch cannot bear fruit by itself, unless it abides in the vine, neither can you, unless you abide in me.* I am the vine; you are the branches. Whoever abides in me and I in him, he it is that bears much fruit, for *apart from me you can do nothing.* . . . If you abide in me, and my words abide in you, ask whatever you wish, and it will be done for you" (John 15:4-5, 7).

Without faith, we make plans according to our strength. Plans are limited in size because we are depending on our resources and abilities. The self-reliant plans of some are larger than those of others due to pride, but each is limited by their abilities.

When we walk by faith God promises to do the impossible.

4. Faith leads us to action.

Faith in God's power drives us toward action, not complacency.

Years ago, when starting an AIDS ministry in South Africa, we were praying about two options: opening a care home or doing home-based care. The care home thrilled me but also terrified me. How could I raise $150,000 plus monthly operating expenses? I couldn't. If it was up to me it would be an epic fail. I distinctly remember this question coming to mind: *Will you trust Me?* God wanted me to step out in faith into something that would utterly fail if He didn't come through. Just as the Israelite priests needed to step into the Jordan River before God parted the waters, we had to step out in faith before God provided. God loves to show His power in our weaknesses! When there is an inner tension that says: *I know I should, but I know I can't*—this is a path to take.

What keeps us complacent? Fear. I am fearful of stepping into the unknown. I don't know about you, but I am rather fond of comfort. (At least the facade of comfort we sedate ourselves with.) In truth, every single day is in His hands, whether we live in Tampa or Tanzania, Toronto or Timbuktu.

Fear of leaving comfort is actually fear of leaving the details in God's hands. Fear is faith's companion. Each new step of faith requires us to trust God in new ways and overcome any fears we have. But we can trust that if God planned the path, He also planned the details. We must face fear with faith.

I saw God do this in our move to Tanzania, and then in the one to Portugal. All the details in these moves were completely unknown. How would we raise the extra funds? Where would we live? Could I actually learn another language? How would our kids adjust? I have often delayed decisions until I "had a peace about it." But I was actually waiting until I "had figured out the details." God didn't ask me to approve the details; He asked me to trust that His plan was best. When I followed God, He worked out all the details far better than I could.

I do still wait for the Holy Spirit to give me peace before proceeding with decisions (2 Corinthians 2:12, 13), but peace only comes after I submit to God's plan. True peace comes in two steps. Step one is the peace that comes from submitting to God's power and trusting Him to work out the details. The second step is the peace that comes from the Holy Spirit confirming a decision in our heart, often in a way that "surpasses all understanding" (Philippians 4:7).

Too often when we say that we "have peace" it is because we think we have a plan or know what tomorrow holds. We are resting in the plan of how we *think* the future will unfold. But we have no idea what tomorrow actually holds. Trusting in God means confidence in a *person*, not just a *plan*. In other words, we find confidence not because we know the plan, but because we know the *person* and are confident any plan He makes is best. We can have peace even if we don't know the plan. Many times God hides His plans from us so we will learn to trust Him.

If we cannot find peace until we know the plan, it's because we are trying to stay in control. We feel we must know and approve of God's plan. We must stop trying to be in control and rest in His control. Peace is not knowing *what* tomorrow holds, it is knowing *who* holds tomorrow. "You keep him in perfect peace whose mind is stayed on you, because he trusts in you" (Isaiah 26:3). Peace is found in knowing a person, not a plan.

The greatest gain is found in the unknown. I want God to use me, but this requires stepping out in faith. If Abraham had stayed in Ur, would we even know his name? Probably not. Abraham was called to follow God, but he wasn't given a destination or the final plan. He had to follow step by step. God simply said to him: "Go . . . to the land that I will show you" (Genesis 12:1).

Like Abraham, we are called to follow God by faith, step by step. We aren't given the entire plan. "Go . . . and behold, I am with you always, to the end of the age" (Matthew 28:19, 20).

Step into the unknown. God has already been there—and He makes a great travel guide.

Hebrews 11 lists the actions of men and women God used in mighty ways. But how were those actions accomplished? By faith. Faith enables us to walk toward our fear because of a greater confidence in God.

What happens when there is a ministry opportunity and I have the desire and gifting to pursue it? I get excited! But this is also where fear creeps in. Fear reminds me of all my inadequacies, of all the logical or logistical reasons why it's not a good idea, and of all the safer options I should pursue. I am fearful when my heart's leading/gifting and my inability intersect. In other words, fear creeps in when it's my area of gifting but it's way beyond my ability. Deep down, I know it's what God wants me to do. I know I should, but I also know I can't.

Fear actually helps. It helps me identify the path in which I must fully trust God instead of myself. I am fearful when presented with an opportunity, and part of me is saying "Yes, this is what you were made to do" while another part is saying "There is no way you can do this!" Every step of faith is a step up. God calls us to harder and harder things. But even though the steps are harder, I learn to trust Him more each time. His past faithfulness gives confidence of His future faithfulness. He is faithful and will carry us through!

One of my mentors, Bruce McDonald, often asks: "What in your life can only be explained as a work of God?" When I walk away from fear, the answer will always be "nothing." When I walk toward fear, God will do things that can only be explained as a work of God.

"Now to him who is able to do far more abundantly than all that we ask or think, according to the power at work within us, to him be glory in the church and in Christ Jesus throughout all generations, forever and ever. Amen" (Ephesians 3:20, 21).

5. Faith leads us forward to the reward.

Keeping our eyes on the destination makes our path less fearful. Why does one path feel more fearful than another? Because we are shortsighted. We are looking at the path instead of the destination. One path looks comfortable, the other looks fearful. But what lies beyond? What's at the end? The path marked "fear" leads to following God wherever He leads. It leads to "Well done, good and faithful servant, enter into the joy of your master"!

It's hard. But it's also worth it.

Here is how this helped me when facing the decision to take the regional director role and move from South Africa to Tanzania. I felt fear knowing the decision would be hard and require massive changes (moving countries, learning a new language, raising more support, and many other things). But my greater fear was looking to the end of my life. I was more afraid that I would get to the end of my life and have God say to me, "I had so much more that I wanted to use you for. If only you had trusted me . . . " My fear of missing out on future rewards was greater than my fear of missing out on temporal comfort.

God is going to work, but He must use willing servants. God used Moses, but fear prevented Moses from becoming God's mouthpiece. God used Aaron instead, and Moses missed a greater opportunity. I fear missing opportunities to follow God more than I fear the unknown or loss of comfort. Sometimes the biggest opportunities are not in change, but in persevering where we are. Often the greatest fruit comes after years in one ministry location. Both persevering and stepping into the unknown require faith.

Faith in the greater rewards helps us lay aside lesser rewards (like the praise of man or comfort) and go after the eternal rewards God has promised. Faith helps us pursue our eternal reward, not our temporal comfort.

When we follow Him in faith, His power will flow through us, and this will result in Him receiving the praise and glory.

WHY DOES FAITH MATTER TO GOD?

Imagine a servant whose job is to proclaim the greatness of the king. This person is to proclaim the king's limitless power, trustworthiness, love, goodness, and promises of great reward to those who follow him.

The servant does tell people about these things, but the servant also always worries when problems arise. Many times he worries about the outcome of things the king has promised. At other times, when things happen that the servant doesn't like, he complains.

Would this honor the king? No. The servant's life destroys the message. The king would rather send servants who have faith because this proves he is trustworthy. If the servant doesn't trust him, why should others?

Servants who get worried or scared about the outcome show a lack of faith in the king's unlimited power. Everyone watches the servant when problems arise. If the servant panics, everyone will think the master doesn't have things under control. Worry makes the king look incompetent and unpowerful.

Why does the servant worry? Because the king may do something he doesn't approve of. So when the servant worries, he is actually concerned about this: that the king is not going to bend his knee to the servant's will or do what the servant thinks is best for his life.

If the servant grumbles or complains, it communicates that he thinks he could do a better job than the king! Who gets the glory? The servant. Complaining steals the king's glory and makes it look like the servant is a better candidate for king than the king himself! Complaining says: "I could do a better job! I am wiser than the king!"

Unbelief and worry make the king look less glorious. They communicate that his power is not strong enough to do what he promised.

On another level, unbelief shows that the servant is not satisfied with the master's current gifts and future promises. The king promised to reward those who seek him.

God's servant needs a life of faith that validates the infinite promises of God and His unwavering trustworthiness. Others need to see the servant living by faith because they can't yet see the promises. Only eyes of faith can see the promises. The carnal eye, however, *can see people living by faith*. By seeing the servant's life of faith they may realize there is something they are not seeing: God's promises.

So who do you think the king will send as an ambassador? A servant who has faith or one who doesn't? He will not use servants who make him look small and weak. He will not use servants who make him look unreliable when they worry about results. He will not use servants who make him look unwise when they complain about events or the king's choices.

Why would the king send a messenger whose life destroys the message?

The king is looking for servants whose lives validate the message.

What kind of servant are you?

FAITH MATTERS BECAUSE IT FULFILLS GOD'S ULTIMATE GOAL: TO GLORIFY HIMSELF

Faith in God's power gives God glory when deeds are accomplished. Paul demonstrated this when he said, "My speech and my message were not in plausible words of wisdom, but in demonstration of the Spirit and of power, so that your faith might not rest in the wisdom of men but in the power of God" (1 Corinthians 2:4, 5).

Faith determines if I will step out in obedience. It also determines who gets the glory.

Faith enables us to trust God to do things that are impossible with human wisdom or power. As other people see us trusting God, they also see that the power is coming from an outside source.

If our primary goal is to bring glory to God, then faith is essential. Faith trusts in His power to accomplish the work, not our power. Rather than our sufficiency and power being seen, God's is. Faith highlights God's faithfulness and dependability.

When I let fear and uncertainty rule my life, I make God look small. Confidence and faith bring glory to God because they show He is powerful enough to do what He says He will.

If we as God's servants don't trust Him to supply our earthly needs or to do what He promised, how will unbelievers think He is trustworthy enough to rest their eternal destiny on Him?

God is looking for servants who trust Him because it shows He is indeed all-powerful, loving, caring, trustworthy, and true.

The messenger validates the message!

What is your life communicating to others?

Chapter 7

THE BARRIER OF UNBELIEF: PART 2

HOW IS THE BARRIER OF UNBELIEF REMOVED SO WE CAN GROW IN FAITH?

Preparing to minister to HIV-positive people in South Africa forced me to face many fears. It revealed areas in which I was not trusting God. At the time, South Africa was the AIDS hotspot of the world. Fueling the spread was a common belief among the Zulu tribe that having sex with a virgin could cure a person from AIDS. Since no one knew who the virgins were, South Africa had the highest rape rate and child/infant rape rate in the world.

And we would be ministering in the townships that caused the brunt of those statistics.

My struggle as a husband and father: would I trust God to take my family into these dangerous places? There was the risk of me, my wife, or kids contracting AIDS. There was also the constant risk of violent crime or rape for my wife and daughters. I knew God could keep us safe just as easily as He kept Daniel safe from the lions. But sometimes God doesn't choose to keep us safe. Wrestling with these truths, I dove deeper in my understanding of the sovereignty of God. Fully resting in the sovereignty and goodness of God is the bedrock of living by faith without fear.

The first day our children joined us at an AIDS support group is one I will never forget. Our girls, ages 4 and 5, walked up and down the aisles greeting HIV-positive patients seated on rickety wooden benches. Many of the people had open cuts or seeping wounds and our girls knew to be careful of this, but we still didn't anticipate all the hugs and handshakes they would get. As HIV-positive patients hug your kids you realize that, while precautions are wise, they are not foolproof. In that moment we had to fully entrust our family to God. He had called us to minister to these people, and He would keep us as safe as He deemed best. We had to trust His heart.

Our natural tendency would be to pull back toward greater safety, but we knew we were exactly where God wanted us. That simple act of faith—bringing what was most valuable to us—showed love to hurting people and opened many doors for the gospel. If we had responded in fear, those doors would have remained shut.

We never lived in a cavalier fashion (I took many precautions), but we also didn't live in fear. To do so, I had to learn to grow in faith.

Through facing these fears, God taught me two key ways to grow in faith:

• Understand the root of unbelief.

• Focus on God and His promises as we exercise our faith.

UNDERSTAND THE ROOT OF UNBELIEF

Over the years I have realized there are two paths that fear and unbelief usually take. Whenever we are thrown into a trial that is outside of our control, it is an opportunity to either live in faith or fear.

Here are two paths fear can take:

1. To fear something is to *fear that God is not in control of that something.*

2. To fear something is to *fear that God's will is not best for our life.*

1. Fear that God is not in control

The first kind of fear is rooted in trusting God's complete sovereignty (His eternal plan and control over all that comes to pass). Most of us believe in our head that God is in control, but what happens when a trial comes? It tests the theology of our heart. Knowing a parachute can prevent you from becoming an omelet is one thing—trusting that parachute enough to jump out of a plane is entirely different. Knowing that God is trustworthy, powerful, and good is one thing—trusting Him in a trial is entirely different.

The storms of life test our theology.

When a trial comes our way, does our heart begin to fear?

Are we concerned with the outcome?

Are we concerned that something will slip past God's watchful care?

Usually, our fear comes because we focus on the storm, not the Lord. We quickly forget that God controls the storms. Like Peter, we must fix our eyes on the Lord and take His hand as we walk through the storms of life.

We remind ourselves that He is in complete control. Practically speaking, we do this when we obey the command "be still and know" that He is God. Not only do we fix our eyes on Him, we also present our requests to God. "I cry out to God Most High, to God who fulfills his purpose for me" (Psalm 57:2).

When we present our requests to God in faith, we are placing our burdens on His back. We must be careful not to try to pick them up again. They were not meant for us to carry!

> *To fear something is to fear that God is*
> *not in control of that something.*

As I applied this truth to my life in South Africa, it meant trusting that God was sovereign over the actions of people. If He wanted to prevent violence, rape, and disease from happening to us, He could do it. There is nothing outside of His control. God regularly brought these words to mind: "To fear something is to fear that God is not in control of that something." God would challenge my heart with this question: *Is the thing you fear outside of my control?* The answer was always the same: no.

This revealed that many times my greater fear was not unbelief in God's sovereignty, it was unbelief in His goodness. I feared He would allow something I didn't want.

2. Fear that God's will is not best for our life

The second kind of fear is rooted in trusting God's goodness. His goodness flows out of His being; He is loving and merciful toward us. When we fear that God may allow something into our life that is not for our good, we are fearing that God is not loving toward us.

We quickly forget that God is acting from an eternal perspective. He knows what will conform us into the person He wants us to be. He knows what is best for our eternal good, not just our present comfort. Any time our comfort is threatened, we begin to fear. Part of this fear is that we love comfort. Our attention and focus are more concerned with improving or maintaining our temporal comfort than improving our eternal joy. So when God, with love, throws us into a trial to provide an opportunity to improve our eternal comfort, we are fearful. We are fearful anytime our temporal comfort is threatened.

To help us combat this fear, we must focus on two things. First, we must "seek the things that are above, where Christ is, seated at the right hand of God. Set your mind on the things above, not on the things that are on earth. For you have died, and your life is hidden with Christ in God. When Christ who is your life appears, then you also will appear with him in glory" (Colossians 3:1-4). When we have a treasure that we cannot lose, we have a confident joy that cannot be shaken.

Second, we must remember that God is acting in love for our eternal good. Trials have a purpose. They are meant for our eternal good. Like a surgeon removing cancer, God is refining our soul by removing sin. Pain is the path to pleasure; we must remember that everything God allows us to endure flows from a loving God. He is a merciful God! "Be merciful to me, O God, be merciful to me, for in you my soul takes refuge; in the shadow of your wings I will take refuge, till the storms of destruction pass by" (Psalm 57:1). We can cling to the mercy of God. As we walk through the storms of life, we can't see what the future holds, but we can hold on to our Father's hand because He sees beyond the storm. He will lead us on a good path. The best path!

To fear something is to fear that God's
will is not best for our life.

The Result

When we fix our eyes on God and trustingly hold His hand through the fog of life, the result is a joy that spills into praise! "I will give thanks to you, O Lord, among the peoples; I will sing praises to you among the nations. For your steadfast love is great to the heavens, your faithfulness to the clouds. Be exalted, O God above the heavens! Let your glory be over all the earth!" (Psalm 57:9-11)

Life is full of trials, but in ministry and missions you will face even more. God desires to refine us; Satan desires to destroy us. How well we learn to walk in faith—rather than in fear—will determine our longevity in ministry and missions.

When we fix our eyes on God—on His complete control over all that comes our way, and on His loving mercy that acts for our eternal good—then we can walk through the storms and fog of life with joyful confidence.

This doesn't mean trials won't hurt, or that we should laugh them off. Rather, we are deeply rooted in unshakable joy while confronting daily pain and loss. We are at peace.

Here are two great truths I've had to work hard to learn: *nothing gets to us that doesn't pass through the hands of God, and nothing passes through His hands that is not for His glory and our eternal good.*

Believing this in your head might take a day. Embedding it in your heart takes a lifetime.

And yet the journey is worth it.

Understanding the root of unbelief is essential to walking by faith.

FOCUS ON GOD AND HIS PROMISES AS WE EXERCISE OUR FAITH

The second key to grow in faith is focusing on God and His promises. I have always wanted my life to glorify God—to live a life that shows God's infinite power and worth so that He gets all the praise, not me. In fact, this was the main reason I went into missions. The Bible is filled with stories of people who God used to show His power. Reading these stories, my heart says, "Lord, use me for your glory. Show your power through me!"

But here is something I missed (or maybe I secretly hoped I would be the exception): When God used people to show His power, what did He use most? Comfort or trials?

Answer: trials.

They are God's most-used tool.

Think about the people in the Bible who God used. He entrusted Job, Joseph, Daniel, Moses, David, Isaiah, Paul, and many others with major trials. Most of the people we remember faced great trials. In fact, we remember them because of how they faced their trials! Had they never faced a major trial, we might not know their names. We know them because they exercised faith in the midst of trials.

This has massive implications if we desire to be used by God for His glory. The last time I checked, the Trinity hasn't announced a change in strategy. God still uses trials. God still uses storms.

So my reality check was this: If I want to be used by God for His glory, I must be prepared for trials. God entrusts us with trials. Lots of them. Paul said that "through many tribulations we must enter the kingdom of God" (Acts 14:22).

Do you want to be used by God?

It's worth it. But it isn't easy.

Why does God use trials so often?

Because of what they do.

Trials are opportunities for faith. They exercise our faith.

Below are some perspective-changers that help us focus on God and His promises while exercising our faith. If you have the courage to follow God wherever He leads, these perspectives will become more than head knowledge. They will become deeply embedded in your heart because, during trials, you will cling to them like a drowning person clinging to a raft. Storms will come, but these truths will keep you afloat.

1. Trials are part of God's work.

God never says "oops." (Credit to my Bible college professor Kelly O'Rear, who often said this.) God is in control of the trials. God is not on His throne wringing His hands waiting for the outcome of events. Even if I can't see how, I can be confident God is working for His glory. This helps me stop worrying about how things are going to work out. My heart is peaceful when I remember that God promises to work for His glory and our eternal good.

Pain is not without purpose. When you have pain, always recall these two verses:

> "Be still, and know that I am God. I will be exalted among the nations, I will be exalted in the earth!" (Psalm 46:10)

> "And we know that for those who love God all things work together for good" (Romans 8:28).

2. Trials put God's power on display.

When God allows me to step into a trial, He may be getting ready to work for His glory. Historically, this is how God prefers to work. Remember Gideon? He started off with an army one-fifth the size of the Midianites—and then God made the odds even worse.

> "The Lord said to Gideon, 'The people with you are too many for me to give the Midianites into their hand, lest Israel boast over me, saying, "My own hand has saved me""" (Judges 7:2).

God uses trials to show that He alone deserves the credit. Trials make it clear to the world that I am not in control. Everyone can see that I don't have the ability or strength to overcome the problem. Therefore, when God works He gets all the glory, not me.

3. Trials prepare me for service—even little trials.

Here is the bad news. When God works in a big way, it often involves one of His servants facing a big trial. So we need to be ready for big storms and trials. How can we prepare? Little trials. I want God to trust me with His big tasks, but God doesn't give us the big tasks without testing us in the little things. Every trial God sends, even our daily frustrations, are meant to test us and help us grow stronger. If I want God to use me for big things, I must pass the little tests. If I don't pass the little tests, why should I expect God to entrust me with greater things?

As I look back over our time in missions, God has continually used trials. If I wasn't in one, I was getting ready to begin one. Just as our physical body grows stronger through the trials of exercise, our soul grows stronger through the trials of life. Without trials our body and soul become weak. Seth Godin made this very apropos comment: "Soldiers realize that it's war that makes generals."[8]

"We rejoice in our sufferings, knowing that suffering produces endurance, and endurance produces character, and character produces hope, and hope does not put us to shame, because God's love has been poured into our hearts through the Holy Spirit who has been given to us" (Romans 5:3-5).

4. Trials sanctify me.

I don't always handle trials well. I think one of the reasons God moved me to Africa for eleven years was to teach me how impatient I really am. When things don't go as planned—traffic seems endless, ministries struggle, paperwork abounds, health suffers—I realize just how impatient I am.

The trials don't cause me to sin by being impatient, angry, or complaining, they simply reveal what is inside. Trials reveal weaknesses. They reveal inner sin. Once I am aware of my weaknesses, I can seek God's help to overcome them. The greatest battle is the internal one. Because of this, God's trials have been His greatest instrument of growth in my life.

"Count it all joy, my brothers, when you meet trials of various kinds, for you know that the testing of your faith produces steadfastness. And let steadfastness have its full effect, that you may be perfect and complete, lacking in nothing" (James 1:2-4).

5. Trials make me depend on God.

God uses trials to turn my dependence fully on Him. He wants me to cling to Him and find peace in Him alone. The greatest battle waged each day for the glory of God is not the one around me—it's the one in me. My sinful heart doesn't want to relinquish control. Trials are God's tool to break my dependence on self so I will trust in Him alone.

Trials and weaknesses keep me from embezzling God's glory. They make it clear that God alone deserves the recognition and honor.

"God chose what is low and despised in the world, even things that are not, to bring to nothing things that are, so that no human being might boast in the presence of God. . . . as it is written, 'Let the one who boasts, boast in the Lord'" (1 Corinthians 1:28-29, 31).

6. Trials show others that God is dependable.

As I go through trials, others are watching. They are watching to see if I respond in faith. Having peace in the midst of *comfort* is normal. Having peace in the midst of trials is not. Trials give me an opportunity to speak about the hope that I have. If I complain or have a bad attitude when facing trials, I forfeit my opportunity to speak of the greatness of God!

God entrusts us with trials so we can be a light. Let's not waste these opportunities.

"But even if you should suffer for righteousness' sake, you will be blessed. Have no fear of them, nor be troubled, but in your hearts honor Christ the Lord as holy, always being prepared to make a defense to anyone who asks you for a reason for the hope that is in you" (1 Peter 3:14, 15).

7. Trials show us and others God's infinite value.

As I go through trials or loss with peace and joy—or lack of it—others are watching. They are watching to see whether I respond in joy. When I have joy in the midst of loss, it shows the world that Jesus is better than what was lost.

Unfortunately, joy in the midst of loss is not my default setting. I think my default is complaining, self-pity, and seeking sympathy. So before I respond in joy, God has to teach me that Jesus is better than anything this world has to offer. He teaches through trials and loss that He alone is my treasure and great reward.

This doesn't mean I laugh things off. Loss hurts—a lot. But my joy is in something that cannot be shaken.

We can feel incredible loss and unshakable joy in God at the same time. Even if we lose everything, God is still enough. Through tears we can say, with Job, "The Lord gave, and the Lord has taken away; blessed be the name of the Lord" (Job 1:21). We can say, with Asaph, "Whom have I in heaven but you? And there is nothing on earth that I desire besides you. My flesh and my heart may fail, but God is the strength of my heart and my portion forever" (Psalm 73:25, 26). We can echo the heart of Habakkuk when we say, "Though the fig tree should not blossom, nor fruit be on the vines, the produce of the olive fail and the fields yield no food, the flock be cut off from the fold and there be no herd in the stalls, yet I will rejoice in the Lord; I will take joy in the

God of my salvation. God, the Lord, is my strength" (Habakkuk 3:17-19).

8. Trials are an opportunity for reward.

God entrusts me with trials as gifts. If I respond to trials in faith and holiness, I can have joy in the fact that I am storing up heavenly rewards. If I respond to trials with fear or complaining, I miss opportunities for reward.

"In this you rejoice, though now for a little while, if necessary, you have been grieved by various trials, so that the tested genuineness of your faith—more precious than gold that perishes though it is tested by fire—may be found to result in praise and glory and honor at the revelation of Jesus Christ" (1 Peter 1:6, 7).

9. Trials may be spiritual warfare.

When we opened the AIDS Care Home in South Africa, we came under attack. On opening day, my wife Heather came down with mononucleosis, and it lasted a year. Days after opening I began suffering from debilitating migraines. Later, Heather needed a serious tumor removed. And then we had a demon-possessed worker and patients—one even attacked Heather.

But I am a little slow. It took another missionary and a Zulu pastor to point out that we were likely facing spiritual warfare. As Westerners, for some reason we are often slow to consider spiritual warfare—at least I was. When our life and ministry are carrying the gospel into spiritually dark places, we are entering Satan's strongholds. He won't leave without a fight.

But I also learned I don't need to fear, because Satan is like a dog on God's leash. He can only do what God allows (remember Job). God may allow Satan to harm me, or even kill me, but it always has a purpose, and it's always for my eternal good. When trials come, I must keep my eyes on God, but I need to be aware of Satan's tactics "so that we would not be outwitted by Satan; for we are not ignorant of his designs" (2 Corinthians 2:11).

Satan wants to discourage us so we give up. He will attack our health, our family's health, and send a myriad of trials to take us out of the fight. Don't let him. Stand firm. Keep your eyes on God. If you are getting bombarded with trials, take heart—it may be because Satan is not happy with your life and ministry!

"Wait for the LORD; be strong, and let your heart take courage; wait for the LORD!" (Psalm 27:14)

"He who is in you is greater than he who is in the world" (1 John 4:4).

"Finally, be strong in the Lord and in the strength of his might. Put on the whole armor of God, that you may be able to stand against the schemes of the devil. For we do not wrestle against flesh and blood, but against the rulers, against the authorities, against the cosmic powers over this present darkness, against the spiritual forces of evil in the heavenly places. Therefore take up the whole armor of God, that you may be able to withstand in the evil day, and having done all, to stand firm. Stand therefore, having fastened on the belt of truth, and having put on the breastplate of righteousness, and, as shoes for your feet, having put on the readiness given by the gospel of peace. In all circumstances take up the shield of faith, with which you can extinguish all the flaming darts of the evil one; and take the helmet of salvation, and the sword of the Spirit, which is the word of God, praying at all times in the Spirit, with all prayer and supplication" (Ephesians 6:10-18).

10. Trials may be for discipline.

Start with the heart. Even though I have listed this one last, this area, in the truest sense, is the place to start. I always begin by examining my heart. God often uses trials or sicknesses to get our attention and reveal sin. As a loving Father He wants to restore our fellowship with Him.

"Do not regard lightly the discipline of the Lord, nor be weary when reproved by him. For the Lord disciplines the one he loves" (Hebrews 12:5, 6).

"Search me, O God, and know my heart! Try me and know my thoughts! And see if there be any grievous way in me, and lead me in the way everlasting!" (Psalm 139:23, 24).

How can we grow in faith?

Changed perspective.

Rather than focusing on trials, we focus on God and His promises as we exercise our faith.

Peter walked on water during the storm because his eyes were on the king, Jesus. When his eyes focused on the storm, he sank like a rock. The storms and trials of life may rage, but our perspective changes everything.

Don't run from trials. Don't fortify your life so you can stay comfortable and safe. In doing so, you'll miss out on being used by God.

Are trials hard? Absolutely! But I would never trade any of my trials because of what God did through them.

Trials and tests are an opportunity to walk by faith—and for God to use us. God entrusts us with trials because He is using us for His glory. He is at work in us, through us, and around us. Take courage. He is working.

THE BIG PICTURE

Because God's goal is to glorify Himself, He is looking for servants who walk by faith. Faith honors God by trusting Him and making Him look great! Whether it be stepping out in faith to follow God or having faith in God in the midst of trials, faith always magnifies God.

If we long to be used by God, we must walk by faith.

The messenger models the message!

What is your life communicating?

Chapter 8

THE BARRIER OF DISOBEDIENCE: PART 1

*Is my holiness today affecting
my usefulness tomorrow?*

*"Now in a great house there are not only vessels of gold and
silver but also of wood and clay, some for honorable use, some
for dishonorable. Therefore, if anyone cleanses himself from what
is dishonorable, he will be a vessel for honorable use, set apart
as holy, useful to the master of the house, ready for every good
work" (2 Timothy 2:20, 21).*

WHAT IS DISOBEDIENCE?

Disobedience is doing what God has told us not to do. Whenever we break any part of His commands, it is disobedience. Just as when a parent tells a toddler not to touch something and they put their pinky finger on the object. That is disobedience. It encompasses completely abandoning God's commands as well as subtly breaking them.

Disobedience also involves more than just our outward acts and our words. We disobey in our mind by thinking about sin and in our heart by desiring sin (which are interconnected). We can break God's commands in our heart without ever lifting a finger or saying a word.

WHAT IS HOLINESS?

Holiness—the centrality and priority of God's person—is part of what sets God completely apart from man. He is entirely pure and His character is the standard for our holiness. "You shall therefore be holy, for I am holy" (Leviticus 11:45).

When we consider our holiness, there are two aspects to consider. The first is our positional holiness. All those who are redeemed by Christ are covered by His blood and therefore God the Father sees us as holy. "But you are a chosen race, a royal priesthood, a holy nation, a people for his own possession, that you may proclaim the excellencies of him who called you out of darkness into his marvelous light" (1 Peter 2:9). Even though we are positionally holy, we must grow in practical holiness day by day.

The second aspect of holiness is our practical daily obedience to God. It is living in right relationship with God, moment by moment, as we walk in His commands. In these next two chapters, this is the primary way that I will be using holiness: our holy obedience to God.

WHY DOES HOLINESS MATTER TO US?

1. God notices our holiness.

Coal miners used to take a canary into mine tunnels with them. If dangerous, undetectable gas levels like carbon monoxide were too high, the canary would die before the miners did.

The canary was an early warning system of toxic gas that signaled to the minors to get out fast.

God already knows our hearts, but our holiness—or lack of it—is somewhat like a dying canary. If we are not growing in holiness, there is a heart problem. Other people may not detect it yet, but it's toxic.

God is concerned about our holiness in all areas of our heart. Notice what God says He is looking for:

"All these things my hand has made, and so all these things came to be, declares the LORD. *But this is the one to whom I will look: he who is humble and contrite in spirit and trembles at my word*" (Isaiah 66:2).

"The LORD has sought out a man *after his own heart*" (1 Samuel 13:14).

"But the LORD said to Samuel, 'Do not look on his appearance or on the height of his stature, because I have rejected him. *For the LORD sees not as man sees:* man looks on the outward appearance, but *the LORD looks on the heart*'" (1 Samuel 16:7).

"For the eyes of the LORD run to and fro throughout the whole earth, to give strong support to those whose *heart is blameless toward him*" (2 Chronicles 16:9).

"Behold, *the eye of the LORD is on those who fear him,* on those who hope in his steadfast love" (Psalm 33:18).

"For *the eyes of the Lord are on the righteous,* and his ears are open to their prayer. But the face of the Lord is against those who do evil" (1 Peter 3:12).

From God's description of how He searches for such hearts you get the impression this type of heart is not common. They are indeed rare.

When God searched Israel He "found David."

Why him?

> "He raised up David to be their king, of whom he testified and said, 'I have found in David the son of Jesse *a man after my heart, who will do all my will*'" (Acts 13:22).

David was not chosen for his appearance, abilities, or anything he could do for God. He was chosen for his heart, which completely loved God and obeyed the will of God.

The Lord is looking for holy hearts. A heart obedient to God's commands is one submitted to Him as king. If my heart has not submitted to the clear commands of God, how will I submit to His leading and guiding in my life?

> "For his eyes are on the ways of a man, and he sees all his steps" (Job 34:21).

2. Holiness makes us useful.

I want to be useful. The following passage shows what makes a servant useful to God: holiness.

> "Now in a great house there are not only vessels of gold and silver but also of wood and clay, some for honorable use, some for dishonorable. Therefore, *if anyone cleanses himself from what is dishonorable,* he will be a vessel for honorable use, set apart as holy, *useful to the master* of the house, ready for every good work" (2 Timothy 2:20, 21).

Holiness doesn't guarantee God will use us, but it does make us useful. Holiness qualifies us to be used by God. Just as an athlete needs many things to qualify for a high-level sports team, holiness qualifies us to be used by God. Not having holiness disqualifies us.

This thought has profoundly affected my life: *My holiness today affects my usefulness tomorrow.*

One of Satan's tactics is to trick us into believing our sins aren't a big deal to God. He wants us to be casual in our fight against sin. He wants us to believe the lie that "one more sin on the pile of your sins won't matter." But it does. Sin not only diminishes our future reward, it also affects our present life. Some time back, this idea of holiness making us useful really hit a nerve with me. I realized my holiness not only affects my eternity, it also affects my tomorrow! When I choose sin, I am choosing to hinder my usefulness. I am letting sin fill an area of my heart that displaces the presence of God and His power in my life. My holiness today affects my usefulness tomorrow.

If we long to be a servant "to whom God looks," we must be holy servants.

When we choose to sin, we choose to hinder our usefulness as servants.

Who we are is more important than what we do. Far too often we're focused on serving God instead of being the right kind of servant, one to be used by God. God is the source of power for all we do, therefore He is unimpressed with our abilities, skills, knowledge, or wisdom. He chooses to give these things to a particular kind of servant, one whose "heart is completely his." Far too often we try to serve God with a divided heart.

Remember Chapter 1, when we saw the connection between God's favor and His presence when Moses spoke to Him.

> "And he said to him, 'If your presence will not go with me, do not bring us up from here. For how shall it be known that I have found favor in your sight, I and your people? *Is it not in*

your going with us, so that we are distinct, I and your people, from every other people on the face of the earth?' And the Lord said to Moses, 'This very thing that you have spoken I will do, for you have found favor in my sight, and I know you by name'" (Exodus 33:15-17).

How does this apply to usefulness? To be useful, we must be filled with His presence. We are only useful to the level that Christ fills us. Apart from Him, we can do nothing.

But for Christ to fill us with His presence, we must walk in holiness. If we allow sin to dwell in us, God will not completely fill us.

Zephaniah reminds God's people to *"Seek the Lord,* all you humble of the land, who do his just commands; seek righteousness; seek humility; perhaps you may be hidden on the day of the anger of the Lord" (Zephaniah 2:3). To seek God is to seek righteousness. To pursue the presence of God is to pursue holiness and righteousness, for He dwells with the righteous. In His holy presence there is no sin. Therefore, the depth of our union with Him is proportional to the sin we allow to remain in our life. To seek Him with our whole heart means to allow Him full reign over us. His presence, not the presence of sin, will fill our heart.

Because God is holy, He will only occupy our heart to the level that we allow Him to push other things out and dislodge sin. Like water, God wants to fill every part of our heart, but He will only fill the space where there is no trash or boulders of sin. May He push out the sin that dwells within.

If we are seeking more of the presence of God, we must seek holiness. Only in pursuing holiness can we experience deeper measures of His fullness as He fills every part of our lives. To seek God is to seek holiness, for seeking holiness results in His presence filling us as we abide in Christ and are filled by His Holy Spirit.

To be useful, we must be filled with His presence. To be filled with His presence, we must be holy. Therefore, holiness is essential to usefulness.

Useful Versus Equipped

Useful is the kind of person we must be if we are going to minister. We must be ready to be used.

"Now in a great house there are not only vessels of gold and silver but also of wood and clay, some for honorable use, some for dishonorable. Therefore, if anyone cleanses himself from what is dishonorable, he will be a vessel for honorable use, set apart as holy, *useful to the master of the house, ready for every good work*" (2 Timothy 2:20, 21).

Being equipped refers to having the knowledge, skills, gifting, and tools we need to minister.

"All Scripture is breathed out by God and profitable for teaching, for reproof, for correction, and for training in righteousness, that the man of God may be complete, *equipped for every good work*" (2 Timothy 3:16, 17).

We need to be *both* ready and equipped.

We need knowledge, skills, gifting, and tools, but these alone do not prepare us. We need to have a holy life that prepares us to minister.

Take a soccer coach as an illustration. The coach has knowledge of how to play the game and even the skills. He is equipped. But if the coach is out of shape, he is not ready to get out on the field. His body and heart aren't able to handle it. Because of this, he would not be a useful player. He could be an amazing coach, but he wouldn't be useful on the playing field. In the same way, our heart and life of holiness make us ready to be used by God. Knowledge alone is useless in God's playing field.

3. God blesses holiness.

Who does God love to bless? Those who honor Him.

"For those who honor me I will honor, and those who despise me shall be lightly esteemed" (1 Samuel 2:30).

"But the one who looks into the perfect law, the law of liberty, and perseveres, being no hearer who forgets but a doer who acts, *he will be blessed in his doing*" (James 1:25).

"But he said, 'Blessed rather are those who *hear the word of God and keep it*'" (Luke 11:28).

"Blessed is the man who walks not in the counsel of the wicked, nor stands in the way of sinners, nor sits in the seat of scoffers; but his delight is in the law of the Lord, and on his law he meditates day and night. *He is like a tree planted by streams of water* that yields its fruit in its season, and its leaf does not wither. In all that he does, he prospers. The wicked are not so, but are like chaff that the wind drives away" (Psalms 1:1-4).

"Blessed are those whose way is blameless, who walk in the law of the Lord! Blessed are those who keep his testimonies, who seek him with their whole heart" (Psalms 119:1, 2).

"Blessed are they who observe justice, who *do righteousness at all times!*" (Psalms 106:3)

"If you know these things, *blessed are you if you do them*" (John 13:17).

If we desire God's blessing on our life and ministries, holiness is essential. Why should we expect God to bless our ministry if we are treasuring sin and following the enemy?

However, this does not mean if we obey God we're guaranteed health, wealth, and prosperity. The blessing of God may come in those forms, but not always. The type of blessing I am referring to is God using us for His glory. In the moment, we may not always see how events are being used for His glory, but one day we will. So our ministry may not have the outward success we hope for, but the true test will be whether God is using us to display His glory in the long term. Some missionaries have planted gospel seeds their entire life only to see a small harvest. The harvest came after their death. God blesses according to His plan and in His time so He gets the glory, not us. If we are pursuing holiness we can trust Him to bless as He sees best.

4. Success is contingent on holiness.

God wants His servants to be the example. They model obedience.

Consider God's command to Joshua. Notice the importance God places not only on following Him in faith, but also in obeying His commands.

As we consider the topic of success, it is important to clarify that biblical success does not refer our own personal definition of success. Success is not determined by the world's definition of success. God is not a cosmic genie who grants us health, wealth, and prosperity if we obey Him. In the following passage, "good success" refers to being used by God to accomplish His plan and purpose. It is God going with us. The opposite of good success is this: God actively opposing us and not going with us.

> "Be strong and courageous, for you shall cause this people to inherit the land that I swore to their fathers to give them. Only be strong and very courageous, *being careful to do according to all the law that Moses my servant commanded you. Do not turn from it to the right hand or to the left,* that you may have

good success wherever you go. This Book of the Law shall not depart from your mouth, but you shall meditate on it day and night, so that you may be careful to do according to all that is written in it. For then you will make your way prosperous, and then you will have good success. Have I not commanded you? Be strong and courageous. Do not be frightened, and do not be dismayed, for the Lord your God is with you wherever you go" (Joshua 1:6-9).

It's not enough to take steps of faith and move forward in ministry. God wants us to follow His commands and His plans. We can't go where God wants us to go while living in disobedience on the journey.

When we follow God, we must follow Him in all things. We must follow with our whole heart.

God's servants and leaders are the first followers. Others are looking to us as an example. We are a visible example of what it means to follow God. God's servants are God's coleaders; we simply share what God speaks to us. But we don't want people to follow us, we want them to *follow us as we follow God.*

A leader's life and words are constant reminders to others of how they should follow God.

Our actions can help or hinder success. The pattern of holiness is a condition of success in fulfilling the vision!

Let's take the time to read the Joshua 1 passage again. This time notice how God connects obedience to success. Especially notice the conditional words. (I'll place them in italics.)

"Be strong and courageous, for you shall cause this people to inherit the land that I swore to their fathers to give them. Only be strong and very courageous, being careful to do according to all the law that Moses my servant commanded you. Do not turn from it to the right hand or to the left, *that you may have good success wherever you go.* This Book of the Law shall not depart from your mouth, but you shall meditate on it day and night, so that you may be careful to do according to all that is written in it. *For then you will make your way prosperous, and then you will have good success.* Have I not commanded you? Be strong and courageous. Do not be frightened, and do not be dismayed, for the Lord your God is with you wherever you go" (Joshua 1:6-9).

God wants us to follow Him! That includes steps of faith to follow His plans, and it includes steps of faith to follow His commands. When we follow God's plans and His commands, God honors and blesses.

We don't earn it, but like Joshua we do have a part in making our way prosperous and finding success—all through obedience. Success is a gift from God, but God loves to give it to those who follow Him with their whole heart.

WHY DOES HOLINESS MATTER TO GOD?

What would happen if the king's servant proclaimed the laws, but he himself disobeyed them? The people would think the king is unworthy of obedience. If the servant doesn't obey, why should they? Disobedience discredits words. No matter how many correct tasks he does, they will be tainted by the wrong. He is evil in heart. A holy servant will obey the king. The king will not seek an unholy, disobedient servant to do His tasks.

1. Holiness is important because it fulfills God's goal: His glory.

God wants the world to see His glory and greatness. Unholy servants detract from His glory. Because of this, God is looking for servants who will not make Him look less glorious.

2. There are deep-rooted problems with disobedience.

These problems show us why holiness is so important to God.

A. Disobedience despises and rejects God's gifts.

"Nathan said to David, 'You are the man! Thus says the LORD, the God of Israel, "I anointed you king over Israel, and I delivered you out of the hand of Saul. And I gave you your master's house and your master's wives into your arms and gave you the house of Israel and of Judah. And *if this were too little, I would add to you as much more*"'" (2 Samuel 12:7-13).

God first reminds David that everything is a gift from His hand. God had greatly blessed David. When David acted in sin, he despised the gifts of the Lord as insufficient. David looked at the gifts God had given but was not satisfied. He wanted something more. David sought satisfaction in sin rather than in God's gifts.

God gives us gifts to enjoy. Sin is seeking satisfaction outside of God's good gifts. It is not being satisfied with what He has given. Sin looks at God's gifts, then casts them aside as worthless.

Holiness cherishes God's good gifts.

B. Disobedience despises and rejects God's Word—His promises and warnings.

"Why have you despised the word of the LORD, to do what is evil in his sight?" (2 Samuel 12:9)

God's Word gives promises, but David wanted sin's promises rather than God's promises. God promises that His gifts will bring lasting satisfaction. Satan and sin also promise satisfaction.

When we sin we despise God's commands. We act with disdain toward God because we reject His promise of joy found in keeping His commandments. It's a true lack of faith that God's gifts are best.

God's Word also gives warnings, but David didn't listen. Rather than listen to God, David listened to the words of Satan and sin.

Not only does sin reject God's promises, it also rejects God's warnings. God warns us about the deceitfulness of sin. When we sin we choose to listen to the voice of Satan and sin, not the voice of God.

Imagine standing at the top of a cliff. Behind you, at the cliff's bottom, are sharp rocks. In front of you, a mountain rises into the clouds. Before us lie good things that we cannot yet see. God's promises are like that mountain rising into the clouds. They tell us what lies ahead and beckon us to keep moving upward.

Picture the cliff with sharp rocks (consequences). There are two kinds of consequences.

There are the natural consequences of sin and loving Fatherly discipline. "Those whom I love, I reprove and discipline, so be zealous and repent" (Revelation 3:19). God gives us both—the natural consequences of sin, and the discipline—to keep us on the path. God's warnings keep us from moving backward.

God hates sin because it is choosing to reject both His promises and His warnings. We take His Word and despise it. Sin is like casting God's Word in the mud as if it were worthless.

Holiness is important because it shows that we believe God at His Word. We trust that God's promises are best instead of sin and Satan's promises.

C. Disobedience despises and rejects God Himself.

"You have struck down Uriah the Hittite with the sword and have taken his wife to be your wife and have killed him with the sword of the Ammonites. Now therefore the sword shall never depart from your house, because *you have despised me*

and have taken the wife of Uriah the Hittite to be your wife"
(2 Samuel 12:9, 10).

Not only did David despise the commandments of Israel's
God, God said that David "despised me." God's commandments
are an expression of the heart of God and His desire; therefore
the two cannot be separated. We reject and despise God Himself
when we reject and despise His commandments. Sin is not simply doing what we want, it is an attack on the person of God. As
David soon said, "I have sinned against the LORD" (2 Samuel
12:13).

Holiness honors God as king in our heart. It puts God on the
throne—not us, and certainly not Satan.

D. Disobedience rejects God as king.

Joseph said, "How then can I do this great wickedness and sin
against God?" (Genesis 39:9)

What is sin against a king? Sin is doing what God tells us not
to do.

When we sin we remove God from the throne of our heart
and climb onto the throne ourself. We decide to do it our way,
not God's way. Obedience is submitting to God, disobedience is
not submitting.

"For the mind that is set on the flesh is hostile to God, for
it does not submit to God's law; indeed, it cannot" (Romans
8:7).

The sinful heart hates to submit to God. It wants to be in control and rises up in defiance against God. Sin does what we want,
not what God wants.

When we sin, we are trying to be king. We are seeking to be
God.

E. Disobedience serves the enemy.

How does God see sin? Sin is choosing to not follow God and, in essence, to follow His enemy.

"Do you not know that friendship with the world is enmity with God?" (James 4:4)

"Submit yourselves therefore to God. Resist the devil, and he will flee from you. Draw near to God, and he will draw near to you. Cleanse your hands, you sinners, and purify your hearts, you double-minded" (James 4:7, 8).

When we sin it is not simply acting as we please. We are rejecting God as our king and following His enemy, who is seeking to destroy Him.

F. Disobedience can disqualify us from serving.

God doesn't want servants who merely outwardly conform. He wants inner worshipers.

"By those who come near me I will be treated as holy, and before all the people I will be honored" (Leviticus 10:3).

We are ambassadors of the Most High God. When His servants disregard His law, it makes God look small. The reason is because when we disregard His laws, we also disregard the Lord Himself.

A clear example of this was when Moses disobeyed God by striking the rock instead of speaking to it as he was commanded to do.

"And the Lord said to Moses and Aaron, 'Because you did not believe in me, to *uphold me as holy in the eyes of the people* of Israel, therefore you shall not bring this assembly into the land that I have given them'" (Numbers 20:12).

Every act of sin is an outworking of a heart of unbelief. To disobey is to disbelieve. To disbelieve is to discredit. We belittle God when we don't believe Him and act in disobedience. When I don't treat Him as holy, it dishonors the Lord.

Notice the painful consequence: "Therefore you shall not bring this assembly into the land."

Disobedience affects our usefulness to God. Disobedience makes God look untrustworthy and unholy, which obscures others' view of His glory.

Therefore, God may choose another servant to do the work, one who will not detract from His glory.

> "The Lord said to Moses, 'Go up into this mountain of Abarim and see the land that I have given to the people of Israel. When you have seen it, you also shall be gathered to your people, as your brother Aaron was *because you rebelled against my word* in the wilderness of Zin when the congregation quarreled, *failing to uphold me as holy* at the waters before their eyes.' . . . So the Lord said to Moses, 'Take Joshua the son of Nun, a man in whom is the Spirit, and lay your hand on him'" (Numbers 27:12, 13, 18).

God is constantly growing us, developing us, and testing us. We don't become holy by our own effort. As God works on us, He is searching for servants who honor Him with their whole heart! God is searching just as water searches. He is looking to flow through hearts that are connected to Him and don't have barriers that resist His power and rule over them.

HOW CAN THE BARRIER OF DISOBEDIENCE BE REMOVED SO WE CAN GROW IN HOLINESS?

We come to this critical question. We all have sin. But those barriers need removed so we can grow in holiness. Probably the best example we can turn to is King David. God described David as a man after His own heart. He was not perfect. David sinned, but he fought against sin, cleansed himself, and sought to follow God with his whole heart.

> "Search me, O God, and know my heart! Try me and know my thoughts! And see if there be any grievous way in me, and lead me in the way everlasting!" (Psalm 139:23, 24)

Consider three parts of these important verses.

1. "Search me, O God, and know my heart!"

David opened himself for God to search and know his entire heart. It's like David is saying: "Here I am. I am not hiding anything." This is so important because we should serve with our whole heart. "With all my heart I have sought Thee; do not let me wander from Thy commandments" (Psalm 119:10).

God wants undivided hearts. He wants our entire heart to be His.

To illustrate this, imagine what would happen if an important visitor came to your house unexpectedly. One of your children—whose daily behavior closely resembles a tornado—has just made their rounds, and the house is now in shambles.

What would you do? You would probably quickly tidy the main rooms but wouldn't bother with the bedrooms. You would simply close the doors. So the back of your house could be an absolute disaster, but the guest would never know.

How often do we treat God like this? We bring Him into the house but leave the back rooms closed. We only open the main rooms and try to hide our sin in the back rooms. When we do this our hearts are not fully His. We are living with divided hearts.

God wants us to open all the doors in our heart. He wants to clean every room, every closet, under every bed. He wants our whole heart to be His.

He wants us to say: "Lord, search my heart. You have full access to my whole life. I am opening all the doors. I am opening all the closets and drawers. I am not going to hide sin from you because I want my whole heart to be yours. I *don't* want to live with a divided heart—serving you with part of my heart and savoring and hiding away sins that I love. Search me, O God!"

God doesn't want servants who outwardly conform; He wants inner worshipers. God doesn't want inner rebels as His servants. He desires all of us.

Remember what sin is? Sin is not only doing what we want. Sin is choosing to reject God's promises, God's warnings, and God Himself. Sin is following the enemy.

When we allow sin to remain, to hide away, it is allowing inner rebellion to go unchecked.

To treat God as holy we must walk in all His ways. Our heart cannot be opposed to Him in our thoughts, actions, or intentions, and then we nonetheless expect to be used by God to challenge others to turn to God and obey Him.

A divided heart does not honor the Lord. It shows that God is less than holy, that He is not glorious enough to demand our entire being.

God wants all of me and all of you. But this is not a hostile takeover; it's a rescue mission. He wants to remove the cancer of our sin and infuse us with new life.

"For God sees not as man sees, for man looks at the outward appearance, but the LORD looks at the heart" (1 Samuel 16:7).

And, once more, remember this critical verse: "For the eyes of the Lord run to and fro throughout the whole earth, to give strong support to those whose heart is blameless toward him" (2 Chronicles 16:9).

God wants the hearts of His people to be completely His. The only way to have this is to freely allow Him to search our heart!

2. "Try me and know my thoughts! And see if there be any grievous way in me."

Try, as used here, is the same word used for testing metals like silver or gold. To test a metal, it is heated. As it melts, the impurities float to the top so they can be scraped away. This process is repeated again and again until the metal is pure.

David opens himself to the Lord and is saying, by his actions: "Purify me. Do what is necessary to purge the sin from my life!"

Sin is like lava in a volcano. It is like a fire in our heart that wants to erupt like a volcano. We don't want it to come out, so what do we do? We try to stop the eruptions. If you cap a volcano, lava will blow out the side of the mountain. If you try to cap your anger by not getting upset at your kids, it will probably blow out in other areas like yelling at your dog or getting mad at other drivers. This happens because we didn't take care of the heart problem. All we did was cap one of the eruptions of sin. If we want to grow in holiness we have to go after the source of the problem.

We have to go after our heart!

"The good person out of the good treasure of his heart produces good, and the evil person out of his evil treasure produces evil, for out of the abundance of the heart his mouth speaks" (Luke 6:45).

With God's help we must seek to have a right heart before God, not just right actions.

God wants to purify my heart. He wants me to be like David and say to Him: "Lord, here is my heart. I know it's going to hurt. But heat me up, reveal my sin, and purify me into your image."

Not only does God want to purify our heart, He wants to purify our thoughts. David says, "Know my *thoughts.*" Before we act out a sin, we must think about it! Thoughts are seeds that grow actions. That which we plant, we also reap. That which Satan or our sin nature plants and we do not uproot will bear the fruit of sin.

All sin starts with a thought. Therefore we must lay our thoughts before the Lord as well as our actions. *If we have a sin problem, we have a thought problem.* God wants to purify our thoughts. In the next chapter we will consider practical steps to allow God to try our thoughts and renew our minds.

3. "Lead me in the way everlasting!"

When we lived in Africa we would sometimes hike in the mountains with our kids. When we did, there were a number of dangerous things to watch for. We especially had to be careful of snakes. South Africa boasts an impressive list of deadly snakes— Black Mamba, Puff Adder, Cape Cobra, Boomslang, Rinkhals, Gaboon Viper, Twig Snake, Mozambique Spitting Cobra, Forest Cobra, and Green Mamba . . . just to name a few.

So how did we walk? I had our kids step where I stepped. I instructed them through the difficult places. Step on logs, not over them, so you don't step on a snake. When we went down or up steep inclines, I showed them where to step. I wanted them to do two things.

1. *Depend on me.* When the path was hard, I was there to take their hand and pull them up. I showed them where to step.

2. *Commit to obey.* Not just sometimes, *all* the time. Step by step. They needed to trust that my way was best.

That is exactly what God wants of us.

Do we walk in only some of His ways? No, we are to walk in all His ways. This thought is so simple, yet life changing, if we apply it.

We are to walk with Him one step at a time.

This redefines daily success. Success is walking with God into and out of each circumstance. It is not what we accomplish or get done. It is to walk in all His ways and follow His commandments. That is success.

God is interested not just with our general direction, but with *every step we take.*

If we truly believe this, it will completely change our daily outlook. God is more interested in my moment-by-moment holiness than my productivity.

In other words, God is more interested in me being patient while I wait in traffic than actually getting somewhere quickly to do something I deem important. God is more interested in me being patient and loving with my family than getting things done. God is more interested in our holiness than anything else.

It is true that we should work hard to serve God. But remember King Saul? Saul disobeyed God, then brought a great sacrifice. God's response to Saul was simple. "To obey is better than sacrifice" (1 Samuel 15:22). We cannot replace obedience with service. Sanctification trumps service.

Let Him lead you day by day, step by step!

THE BIG PICTURE

God is looking. He is searching the world! When He looks at your heart, does He find an open house He can have full control over? He is looking for those whose heart is completely His. As previously mentioned, we can't change our heart in our own strength. We can't make our heart completely His. God is the one who gives us the strength to battle sin and even the desire to do so. This is why David opens his heart to God and asks for help in being changed. As God finds these receptive hearts, He pours out more of His power! If you truly desire to be used by God, have this heart on a daily basis!

Consider again Paul's powerful words to Timothy:

"Now in a great house there are not only vessels of gold and silver but also of wood and clay, some for honorable use, some for dishonorable. Therefore, if anyone cleanses himself from what is dishonorable, he will be a vessel for honorable use, set apart as holy, useful to the master of the house, ready for every good work" (2 Timothy 2:20, 21).

"If" is a contingent word.
If we cleanse our heart, we will be useful to the Master.
If we cleanse our heart, we will be a vessel for honorable use.
If we cleanse our heart, we will be ready for every good work.
Our holiness today affects our usefulness tomorrow.
Here is how this promise can help us battle against sin.
Sin works on our desires.

In addition to trying to fight sin in our own strength, another reason we're often defeated by sin is that we try to battle sin with only our thoughts and judgments.

We mentally try to talk ourselves out of sinning. But sin is deceitful and will trick our minds.

One of the ways we must battle against sin is with a spiritual desire for God and holiness. We seek that which we desire. The greater our spiritual desire, the greater our pursuit of holiness and fellowship with God. Our part in growing this desire is by meditating on and memorizing God's Word. As we do, God grows the desire through His Holy Spirit and transforms us by His power.

Memorize the promises of God! Your usefulness is affected by your holiness. When sin tempts your heart with its desires, battle against it with the desire to be a vessel for honorable use, useful to the master, ready for every good work. Battle against sin with a desire to know and fellowship with God.

Battle against sin with a desire for a *life* that magnifies God, not just a ministry that magnifies God. Fight sin's desires with godly desires. Fight Satan's promises and the promises of sin with God's promises. "Fight promises with promises."[9]

God is searching for people whose hearts desire to please Him more than anything else. When He looks at you, does He find such a heart?

Are there barriers in your life hindering Him from flowing through you?

If yes, what steps do you need to take as you fight to remove those barriers?

Chapter 9

THE BARRIER OF DISOBEDIENCE: PART 2

Is my mind dwelling on sin or truth?

"Finally, brothers, whatever is true, whatever is honorable, whatever is just, whatever is pure, whatever is lovely, whatever is commendable, if there is any excellence, if there is anything worthy of praise, think about these things" (PHILIPPIANS 4:8).

During one of our visits to the game park in South Africa, we came across a bull elephant in musth who was blocking the road. (Musth is a condition in which a bull is highly aggressive; the period is marked by a large rise in reproductive hormones and secretion areas on the side of the bull's head.) We decided to keep a safe distance until the bull had finished eating and moved on. Thirty minutes later, however, he was still there. In what felt like slow motion, things began to turn dangerous. In my rear view mirror I saw an entire herd of female and baby elephants rounded the corner behind us. We were trapped with a herd behind us, a bull elephant in front of us, and dense trees on both sides of the road. To make matters worse, the bull elephant decided he wanted to get to the females behind us and began a mock charge at our vehicle.

After a couple of mock charges he moved off to the side of the road. This was the first opportunity we had to get past him, so I floored the gas. Trying to stay as far from the elephant as possible, I veered off the road, driving over bushes and eight-foot-tall trees. Despite an elephant's size, when they want to move, they can really move. He crossed the road like lightning and rammed his tusks through the door, lifting one side of the vehicle three feet off the ground. I kept the gas floored. When the engine's turbo kicked in we surged forward and pulled free from the tusks. Had the turbo not kicked in, he would have flipped the vehicle and could have easily killed us.

The mental image of a charging elephant close enough that we could touch is a memory that will never be erased. Let's just say the entire thing left quite an impact. That day I learned exactly how to identify an elephant in musth. On future visits, whenever I saw or smelled an elephant in musth, I didn't wait around for photos.

Just like that elephant, sin is extremely dangerous. We may think we are safe to get close, but sin wants to destroy us. Allowing sin into our mind puts us seconds away from attack. In a flash, our world can be turned upside down.

THE BATTLE

Sin and Satan are deceitful. They will trick us. Their desire is to destroy us, our testimony, our ministry, our family . . . our life. Whether we know it or not, we are in a battle for our life. We need to take the battle seriously! "Be sober-minded; be watchful. Your adversary the devil prowls around like a roaring lion, seeking someone to devour" (1 Peter 5:8).

When Satan failed to entice Jesus to sin, what happened? "He departed from him until an opportune time" (Luke 4:13). He left, but he was waiting for a better time to return. The war is never over on this side of eternity. Satan wants to lull us into comfort and complacency—and that's when he strikes.

We must be watchful!

Not only does Satan battle for control of our heart, he battles for our mind. With these warnings, here are some additional thoughts on sin and how we can battle against it taking root in our life.

THE MIRAGE OF SIN

Everyone wants to be happy. What people base their happiness on varies greatly, but people pursue happiness in nearly everything they do. One person pursues it by accomplishment, another by laziness. One by wealth, another by simplicity. One by power, another by pleasure.

This world is like a desert and sin is like a mirage. Sin looks like it will satisfy, but the mirage turns to sand in our mouth. Sin can never satisfy or quench our thirst.

Many times we will pursue the same mirage, over and over, with the same disappointing results. Why?

Why do we pursue the mirages? If we only do what we believe will make us happy, why do we pursue something or make a decision that leads to emptiness?

Why do we pursue the same sin over and over when it clearly doesn't satisfy us or make us happy?

Why do we do something and then say to ourselves, "I knew better than that"? If we knew better, why did we do it?

I see two important reasons:

1. We are deceived by the lies of sin and Satan.

2. The more we do a sin, the easier it becomes.

1. We are deceived by the lies of sin and Satan.

When Satan came to Eve in the garden, he lied.

How did he lie? Did Satan confuse Eve, or did he use the lie to deceive her about what would make her happy (her desires)?

He deceived her.

Satan wants us to want sin.

He tells us the same lie over and over: "This will make you happier than God's way." Such a lie creates doubt in God's goodness, His plan, and that His commands are best. When this happens, sin starts looking like a good idea.

Practically speaking, what does this look like? An idea, or thought, pops into your head. At that point it isn't a sin. It's a lie: *This will make me happy.* At that moment we can choose to shut that thought off, or we can choose to dwell on it.

When we choose to dwell on it, the lie is like a seed planted in our brain. It will begin to grow, and sin's desire is to take over and consume and destroy us. Sin is never happy staying small. It always wants to be the worst it can be. One look of lust wants to become adultery. One scornful or vengeful thought wants to grow to murder. One greedy thought wants to consume our life.

When we allow a thought to stay, we welcome sin in our mind.

2. The more we do a sin, the easier it becomes.

Not only does sin affect our heart, it also affects our physical brain. When a thought enters our brain we choose to dwell on it and let it remain, or we make efforts to push it out. At the initial point, it's just a thought; it's not part of us. When we choose to dwell on it and think about it, it becomes part of us. We literally wire it into our brain pathways. "Neurons that fire together wire together. In other words, neurons that repeatedly activate in a particular pattern are statistically more likely to fire in that same pattern the more they are activated."[10] The more we think those thoughts, the more they become wired in our brain.

If we think about good things, we wire our brain to be healthy. If we think negative thoughts that are not trusting God at His Word, or sinful thoughts, our brain will not be healthy.

Why? Because it becomes easier and easier to stay in negative thoughts, and this makes our brain unhealthy and our spirit empty because it is not living as God intended.

An example: I was out hiking recently and at first the path was wide and well worn. The grass and bushes were trampled down, and it was wide enough for a few people to walk side by side. Farther down the path, however, it narrowed and was just wide enough for one person. Finally, near the end, where no one had walked for some time, I had to turn sideways to keep the thorns from catching my pants.

That path is like the pathways in our brain. The more we walk down sin's path, or in an incorrect way of thinking, the easier that path becomes. The path gets wider. The only way to stop it is to stop going down that path! We need to start creating new pathways and let those old ones grow over. Just like a physical path, when we don't go down a pathway for a while, it grows over.

As Luther said, "You cannot keep birds from flying over your head but you can keep them from building a nest in your hair."

HOW CAN WE CHANGE OUR BRAIN?

"Rejoice in the Lord always; again I will say, rejoice. Let your reasonableness be known to everyone. The Lord is at hand; do not be anxious about anything, but in everything by prayer and supplication with thanksgiving let your requests be made known to God. And the peace of God, which surpasses all understanding, will guard your hearts and your minds in Christ Jesus. Finally, brothers, whatever is true, whatever is honorable, whatever is just, whatever is pure, whatever is lovely, whatever is commendable, if there is any excellence, if there is anything worthy of praise, think about these things.

What you have learned and received and heard and seen in me—practice these things, and the God of peace will be with you" (Philippians 4:4-9).

From this passage there are four important ways we can change our brain to help battle sin.

1. Rejoice in God. Always.

"Rejoice in the Lord always; again I will say, rejoice" (Philippians 4:4).

When are we to rejoice? Always. There is no circumstance, no matter how dark it seems, in which you can't find a reason to rejoice. Why? Because our joy isn't based on circumstance. Circumstances change. Our joy is based on God, who doesn't change.

Where are we looking to find our joy? The choice is simple: in circumstances or in Christ. The reason this is so important is because sin always starts with dissatisfaction. We aren't happy with God or His gifts, so we seek satisfaction in sin. If our heart is rejoicing in Christ, we won't be looking for satisfaction in other things.

2. Be thankful for all of God's gifts.

"Do not be anxious about anything, but in everything by prayer and supplication with thanksgiving let your requests be made known to God" (Philippians 4:6). Notice Paul says that thanksgiving should replace anxiety.

Here is what happens when we are anxious:

Anxiety is our body's inbuilt wake-up call that alerts us against danger. When fear sets in, our body releases hormones that create the fight or flight responses, and we react likewise. The brain doesn't get much time to analyze the right or wrong when the adrenaline rush begins . . .

In the book *Grateful Brain*, author Alex Korb (2012) said that our mind cannot focus on positive and negative information at the same time.[11]

Anxiety and thankfulness cannot operate at the same time. If we are being thankful, we will not be anxious. If we are struggling with anxiety, we can begin to practice thankfulness by setting our mind on things we have to be thankful for. We can be thankful for our current gifts and future hope.

Thankfulness for all of God's gifts and future promises is also a protection against the temptation to sin. Satan's greatest lie is that what God has given us or promised to give in the future is not best for us. He wants us to despise the gifts and distrust the giver. If we are thankful for the gifts and promises, our heart will not be as easily tempted to turn to Satan's and sin's promises.

Satan's first entry point is to create doubt in the goodness of God's gifts and promises. If he can get us to doubt the gifts, we will doubt the giver. A thankless heart is open to Satan's attacks.

If we do have a request, we should come to God with that request in prayer, not turn to sin or Satan. We shouldn't take it upon ourselves to seek satisfaction outside God's commands or listen to Satan's lies about where to seek satisfaction.

3. Be aware when you are lacking peace.

"And the peace of God, which surpasses all understanding, will guard your hearts and your minds in Christ Jesus" (Philippians 4:7).

When we are not at peace, Satan is most likely to attack by planting a thought in our mind. Without peace we open ourselves to sin and Satan. Peace will guard our heart and mind.

What does it look like when we are not at peace?

Someone shared an acronym I found easy to remember.

We are easily tempted to BLAST into sin when we are:

Bored
Lonely
Angry
Stressed
Tired

I also added a couple letters: BLASTHH (the H's are silent!).

Hungry
Hurried

If you are in one of those states, beware! Peace doesn't come by holding onto our problems and trying to fix them, but by turning our problems over to God. God's peace goes beyond understanding.

If we think we must figure out the answers or fix our problems to find peace, we are wrong. God can give us peace when we don't yet have the answers. Peace isn't based on circumstances; it's based on the *One who controls the circumstances.* It isn't based on things that change, but on God, who never changes. In a changing world one thing never changes: God.

Don't seek peace in circumstances but in the Creator.

4. Think on truth.

"Finally, brothers, whatever is true, whatever is honorable, whatever is just, whatever is pure, whatever is lovely, whatever is commendable, if there is any excellence, if there is anything worthy of praise, think about these things" (Philippians 4:8).

In this verse, I used to focus more on the purity and excellence rather than on the "whatever is true." But I began to wonder: why did Paul start with "whatever is true"? I always thought to myself: Of course I think about what is true. But then God reminded me that *everything* Satan and sin throw at us is mixed with a lie. It's a lie that says: *God isn't giving you what's best. This path would be better.* Satan's and sin's goal is to plant a thought in our mind so we begin to distrust God. Paul started with truth because it affects all our thoughts. We must evaluate if our thoughts are true or tainted with a lie.

It made me realize that Satan's number one tactic is to plant thoughts in our mind like seeds that grow into full-blown sin and distrust of God. This means one of the best ways to battle sin is to battle the first thought from taking root. This keeps thoughts from even having the *opportunity* to grow. Each time the lie "this will make you happy" comes to mind, quote Scripture and remind yourself of truth.

Satan tries to plant lies like a beachhead in a war to gain access to your mind. Don't let the thought stay there for even a moment! A beachhead doesn't mean an instant defeat; it's just that: a beachhead. In this case, it is a small victory that Satan wins. From that beachhead he can launch multiple attacks. But he doesn't have to win.

The first moment a thought enters is the easiest time to push it out. Sin and our thoughts are like a huge rock at the top of a mountain. Satan wants to push that rock to the bottom. When is the easiest time to stop it? As soon as it starts. God does promise to "provide the way of escape" from sin, but we should not presume that the way of escape is after we've dwelt on sin (1 Corinthians 10:13). Imagine stepping in front of a boulder after it is halfway down a mountain. When we dwell on sin in our mind, that's essentially what happens. It's no wonder we get flattened by sin. We must attack when the *first thought* enters our mind. We must "take every thought captive to obey Christ" (2 Corinthians 10:5). As we do this, we retrain our brain and renew our mind in His image!

Replace lies with truth. When temptation arises, immediately speak this truth to yourself: "This is a mirage, and it wants to destroy me."

PRACTICAL STEPS

1. Identify the things you struggle with most.

These could be:

- Thoughts that often come to mind

- Sins you often act out

- Feelings you are having (examples: anger, discouragement, depression)

Writing out your identified areas is helpful in owning the problem. Until you identify a problem you want to fight with God's help, it will continue to haunt you.

2. Memorize a few key verses that combat the lie Satan tells you.

David said, "I have stored up your word in my heart, that I might not sin against you" (Psalm 119:11).

Putting God's Word in our mind and meditating on important Scriptures creates new pathways in our mind and shows us the right path.

3. Whenever the tempting thought enters your mind, immediately replace it with the verse. Don't let the thought stay.

Replace the lie with truth. Remember the example of Jesus when He responded to Satan. He replaced the lie with truth.

When you use "the sword of the Spirit, which is the word of God" (Ephesians 6:17) to battle the lies of Satan, you are resisting "the devil, and he will flee from you" (James 4:7).

4. Use the acronym STRESS to check your battle readiness.

Satan hits us from different angles. Sometimes we are more vulnerable to temptation in different areas. When temptation arises, conduct a weapons and armor check as you enter battle.

Set your mind on God, Scripture, the things above, and this truth: sin is a mirage and wants to destroy you.

Thankfulness for all God is, has given, and promises to give will help guard you.

Rely on God's strength to battle sin.

Engage the help of others (accountability).

Submit fully to God—body, mind, and heart.

Satisfaction in God and His promises is so crucial.

BIG PICTURE

There is a battle for your soul, and it starts in your mind. Every day we must wake up and prepare for battle.

Former Navy SEAL officer Jacko Willink shared his soldier's mind-set in an interview:

> "For me, when I wake up in the morning and I don't know why, I'm thinking about the enemy and what they're doing ... there's a guy that's in a cave somewhere and he's rocking back and forth and he's got a machine gun in one hand and a grenade in the other hand, and he's waiting for me and we're going to meet. When I wake up in the morning, I'm thinking to myself: what can I do to be ready for that moment which is coming, which is coming."[12]

Just as a soldier daily prepares for war, we must prepare to be attacked by our enemy. There is a spiritual battle going on, and Satan is plotting to take us out.

Like a sniper, Satan patiently waits to fire his lies at us at "an opportune time" (Luke 4:13). We must be always watching and ready. We must prepare our heart and mind "to be ready for that moment which is coming, which is coming."

Chapter 10

THE BARRIER OF PRIDE

Am I embezzling glory?

"But this is the one to whom I will look: he who is humble and contrite in spirit and trembles at my word" (ISAIAH 66:2).

WHAT IS PRIDE?

Pride is when our heart exalts itself and desires to be seen and praised by others. Pride can manifest itself in different ways. Boasting is how pride is manifested in those who delight in their strength. Self-pity is how pride is manifested in those who delight in their sacrifice. Both savor the recognition of others. John Piper reminds us, "The reason self-pity does not look like pride is that it appears to be so needy. But the need arises from a wounded ego. It doesn't come from a sense of unworthiness, but from a sense of unrecognized worthiness. It is the response of unapplauded pride."[13]

WHAT IS HUMILITY?

Humility is an attitude of lowliness based on a proper understanding of our place before God. It is gladly submitting as a creature to our Creator.

WHY DOES HUMILITY MATTER TO US?

1. Humility catches God's eye.

God is looking to use humble people. As it is so important, let's read and think again about the verse I used to start this chapter.

> "'All these things my hand has made, and so all these things came to be,' declares the LORD. 'But this is the one to whom I will look: he who is humble and contrite in spirit and trembles at my word'" (Isaiah 66:2)

Humility doesn't guarantee that God will use us; it makes us useful. If we are proud, it disqualifies us from some service. Just as with holiness, humility qualifies us to be used by God. Our humility today affects our usefulness tomorrow.

As with the barriers of unbelief and disobedience, when pride is removed from our life God will bless us according to His desires. We cannot assume that if we are humble God must use us. Ironically, to do so is to exhibit pride.

When God has a plan He wishes to unfold, He looks for a humble servant to use. If we desire to be used, humility helps us be seen by God. This is counterintuitive. How do we normally try to get noticed? We seek to draw attention to ourselves or our actions. Like little children, we say, "Did you see what I did?" or "Watch this!" We try to draw God's attention to how great we are. God is unimpressed. He is looking for servants who are unimpressed with themselves and only impressed by Him. God's eye is drawn to those who are humble, not to those who are proud.

2. God delights in humility.

If we desire to please God, humility is the pathway.

"He has told you, O man, what is good; and what does the Lord require of you but to do justice, and to love kindness, and to walk humbly with your God?" (Micah 6:8)

"Thus says the Lord: 'Let not the wise man boast in his wisdom, let not the mighty man boast in his might, let not the rich man boast in his riches, but let him who boasts boast in this, that he understands and knows me, that I am the Lord who practices steadfast love, justice, and righteousness in the earth. For in these things I delight,' declares the Lord" (Jeremiah 9:23, 24).

"For though the LORD is high, he regards the lowly, but the haughty he knows from afar" (Psalm 138:6).

Humility pleases God because it is the correct posture for us as created beings. When we are proud and exalt ourselves, we are trying to receive recognition we don't deserve. If we wish to please God, humility is the only way. God hates pride, and it distances us from Him.

3. God blesses the humble.

God's pleasure is not merely passive delight. He also pours out of His favor by actively *helping* the humble. These verses show us the path to God's favor is the path of humility.

"Toward the scorners he is scornful, but to the humble he gives favor" (Proverbs 3:34).

"Before destruction a man's heart is haughty, but humility comes before honor" (Proverbs 18:12).

"God opposes the proud, but gives grace to the humble" (James 4:6).

"For thus says the One who is high and lifted up, who inhabits eternity, whose name is Holy: 'I dwell in the high and holy place, and also with him who is of a contrite and lowly spirit, to revive the spirit of the lowly, and to revive the heart of the contrite'" (Isaiah 57:15).

"The fear of the Lord is instruction in wisdom, and humility comes before honor" (Proverbs 15:33).

Ministry success isn't a result of our ability, it's a result of God's blessing. God delights to bless the humble. How God blesses is according to His plan, but humility makes blessing a possibility.

4. God promises to oppose the proud.

Just as God's pleasure is not merely passive delight, He also pours out trouble on the proud. God is not neutral toward the proud; He is *actively* against them. When we walk in pride, we go to war with God!

"Toward the scorners he is scornful, but to the humble he gives favor" (Proverbs 3:34).

"God opposes the proud, but gives grace to the humble" (James 4:6).

"Pride and arrogance and the way of evil and perverted speech I hate" (Proverbs 8:13).

"Everyone who is arrogant in heart is an abomination to the Lord; be assured, he will not go unpunished" (Proverbs 16:5).

"The haughty looks of man shall be brought low, and the lofty pride of men shall be humbled, and the Lord alone will be exalted in that day. For the Lord of hosts has a day against all that is proud and lofty, against all that is lifted up—and it shall be brought low.... And the haughtiness of man shall be humbled, and the lofty pride of men shall be brought low, and the Lord alone will be exalted in that day" (Isaiah 2:11, 12, 17).

"Now I, Nebuchadnezzar, praise and extol and honor the King of heaven, for all his works are right and his ways are just; and those who walk in pride he is able to humble" (Daniel 4:37).

Pride was the sin of Satan.

"You said in your heart, 'I will ascend to heaven; above the stars of God I will set my throne on high; I will sit on the mount of assembly in the far reaches of the north; I will ascend above the heights of the clouds; I will make myself like the Most High'" (Isaiah 14:13,14).

When we are proud we choose to forfeit the possibility of blessing because God will oppose us. If we want to live and minister in a way that pleases God and is in alignment with Him, we must walk in humility. We must carefully examine our heart so pride does not creep in and sabotage our life and ministry. When we walk in pride, we walk alone. When we walk in humility, we walk with God.

WHY DOES HUMILITY MATTER TO GOD?

Imagine a servant who builds a name for himself instead of his king. The servant sets up a little throne for himself. He doesn't take all the glory, but he does take some of it. Would this servant honor his king? No. The glory belongs to the king, not the servant. Any glory the servant takes is stolen from the king. The king will not seek a proud servant to do his tasks because he knows the servant will wrongfully take the glory that instead belongs to him.

> *Humility matters to God because it fulfills*
> *God's ultimate goal: to bring Himself glory.*

God wants the world to see His glory and greatness, not to have servants trying to be noticed and stealing the glory He deserves. Thus, God is looking for servants who will not get in the way of His glory being seen. In addition, God may use circumstances that humble His servants by revealing their weaknesses so He gets all the glory.

BIBLICAL EXAMPLES OF GOD BLESSING THE HUMBLE

Gideon

When thirty-three thousand Israelites joined to fight, God said it was too many.

"The Lord said to Gideon, 'The people with you are too many for me to give the Midianites into their hand, *lest Israel boast over me, saying, "My own hand has saved me"'"* (Judges 7:2).

After only ten thousand remained, the Lord said, "The people are still too many" (Judges 7:4).

When it was completely impossible by man's standard, God said, "With the three hundred men who lapped [water, in a test created by God] I will save you" (Judges 7:7).

The reason God reduced their number was so that no one would "boast over me." God wants His glory to be seen, and He doesn't want us getting in the way or stealing it. To let His glory be more clearly seen He uses humble servants and often weak servants so that everyone can see it was only His power that accomplished the work!

The Israelites being freed from Egypt

"The Lord your God, who brought you out of the land of Egypt, out of the house of slavery, who led you through the great and terrifying wilderness . . . *that he might humble you* and test you, to do you good in the end. *Beware lest you say in your heart, 'My power and the might of my hand have gotten me this wealth.'* You shall remember the Lord your God, for it is he who gives you power to get wealth, that he may confirm his covenant that he swore to your fathers, as it is this day" (Deuteronomy 8:14-18).

Paul

"*So to keep me from becoming conceited* because of the sur-passing greatness of the revelations, a thorn was given me in the flesh, a messenger of Satan to harass me, to keep me from becoming conceited. Three times I pleaded with the Lord about this, that it should leave me. But he said to me, 'My grace is sufficient for you, for my power is made perfect in weakness.' Therefore I will boast all the more gladly of my weaknesses, so that the power of Christ may rest upon me" (2 Corinthians 12:7-9).

Paul's thorn kept him humble and kept God glorified.

Our calling

"For consider your calling, brothers: not many of you were wise according to worldly standards, not many were pow-erful, not many were of noble birth. But God chose what is foolish in the world to shame the wise; God chose what is weak in the world to shame the strong; God chose what is low and despised in the world, even things that are not, to bring to nothing things that are, *so that no human being might boast in the presence of God.* And because of him you are in Christ

Jesus, who became to us wisdom from God, righteousness and sanctification and redemption, so that, as it is written, 'Let the one who boasts, boast in the Lord'" (1 Corinthians 1: 26-31).

If God chooses to use us so that we will not be proud and boastful, we must be very careful to battle pride.

PHOTOBOMBING GOD

We all probably know a photobomber. This type of person loves to wait for the perfect moment to be the center of attention. Not happy to stay on the sidelines, they want to draw attention to themselves.

Most photobombers are just goofing off, and everyone gets a laugh . . . the first time. But what about persistent photobombers? You know, the ones who won't quit? After a few ruined photos, you look directly at them and say, "Stop photobombing!"

I think God must feel like this every day.

Far too often, we photobomb God. We want to be noticed in the picture of His glory.

He is putting His glory on display for the world to see, and we get in the way! Sure, God is still in the picture, but the picture is ruined. We aren't supposed to be the center of attention. God is!

God isn't laughing. We can be just like the photobomber who won't quit. Day after day we keep grabbing a little attention here and there. We want others to notice us and what we do.

Why does God hate it when we photobomb Him?

Photobombing God goes against His ultimate goal. God's ultimate goal is to put His glory on display.

Photobombing God also goes against our purpose, which is pointing others to God's greatness. We never add to God's glory; we are just here to help others see His glory. When we photobomb God we get in the way of His glory being seen. We are opposing God's ultimate goal!

This is why God speaks so much against pride. It is no wonder God is opposed to the proud—they are opposed to Him! Pride gets in the way of God's glory, but not forever. God will bring all pride crashing down. Isaiah 2:17 says, "And the pride of man will be humbled, and the loftiness of men will be abased, and the Lord alone will be exalted in that day."

EMBEZZLING GLORY

Another way to illustrate what happens when we photobomb God is to think about the act of embezzling. We are supposed to help others see His glory. Any glory we take is embezzled. We have stolen it from God! What makes embezzling so terrible is an embezzler puts on a good face while going to work each day, yet he is secretly robbing the one he pretends to serve. When we take glory for ourselves, we are embezzlers. We put on a good face while serving God day by day, all the while taking some glory and recognition for ourselves. It is embezzled from God in the very act that is supposed to give Him glory.

How deceitful our pride can be!

Like the servant who sets up a little throne for himself, we often serve God as a means of serving ourselves. In our service we become proud of our accomplishments or sacrifice. We may even be proud of our humility!

We may not take all the glory, but we take a little and savor it like a morsel in our mouth. We may try to get glory from fellow servants telling us how great a servant we are.

God says that taking glory is so serious it is trading your future reward for the recognition of man!

"Beware of practicing your righteousness before other people in order to be seen by them, for then you will have no reward from your Father who is in heaven. Thus, when you give to the

needy, sound no trumpet before you, as the hypocrites do in the synagogues and in the streets, that they may be praised by others. Truly, I say to you, they have received their reward. But when you give to the needy, do not let your left hand know what your right hand is doing, so that your giving may be in secret. And your Father who sees in secret will reward you" (Matthew 6:1-4).

Do I want the "well done" of God? If so, I need to stop pursuing the "well done" of men.

To help me do this better, I often ask myself a few questions to evaluate my heart.

1. Am I serving God to be seen by others?

2. Is the *way* I am doing my service almost entirely to be seen? (Think of the Pharisees, who prayed on the street corner or sounded the trumpet when giving money.) The actions may be right, but if I am positioning myself to be seen by others, they are wrong.

3. Would I serve even if nobody saw me?

We must not position ourselves to be seen by others. We must desire to be seen by God alone. The praise and notice of others is meaningless. We may not set up a large throne in front of God, but do we set up little thrones by positioning ourselves to be seen by others? Our pride loves to be seen, noticed, and praised. Examples? We may try to be noticed in some small way for our preaching, our possessions, our kindness, our sacrificial giving of time or money, and other similar efforts.

Many times we do not see ourselves as proud because we compare ourselves to others who are more proud than we are. We say to ourselves that we are not proud because we do not try to raise ourselves as high as others. Pride takes many forms. Some take pride in *not being proud;* that is, they are proud that they are not outwardly proud! They don't drive a fancy car or have the latest technology, but they are proud of this and, in fact, they try to be seen by others for their lack of material things and lack of pride. But pride is the very thing that causes them to want to be seen by others.

One man's pride can push him to amass wealth or rule a country. Another man's pride may push him to live poorly, or live to the level that he is perceived as great. But in the end, each is seeking to be seen for something.

We must ask ourselves: am I doing this to be seen by others, or am I happy to be seen only by God? We may not be outwardly seeking praise, or to be noticed, but what does our heart desire?

Pride is deceitful because it takes many forms, but this one thing never changes: pride longs to be known for something. We want others to remember us by some characteristic; we want to build a name for ourselves. But when we do this we are not building a name for God. We are using our interaction with others to impress them with ourselves. Do we desire others to be impressed with us, or with God? We can deceive ourselves by using our knowledge of God to build a name for ourselves so that others are impressed—more with our knowledge of God than they are with God!

HOW DO WE PHOTOBOMB GOD?

There are many ways we photobomb God.

- Trying to be seen by others and noticed for what we have done or accomplished.

- Wanting others to like us and what we do.

- Seeking attention on social media.

- Trying to build a personal fan club.

Let's look at that last one: pride is like trying to build a personal fan club. It watches our every move and cheers us on, validating our perceived greatness. It also watches others to see if they notice our perceived greatness, to see if we can entice them to join our little fan club.

Maybe that isn't you. Maybe instead you are consumed with thoughts of your inadequacy or sacrifice for God. Pride can also seek to be noticed by others for our weakness, struggles, busyness, suffering, or sacrifice. Here, *pride throws a personal pity party.* Getting support and encouragement isn't wrong; we are told to encourage one another. But wanting others to join our personal pity party is rooted in pride.

When pride is at work, we aren't trying to help people see God. We're trying to be seen. Pride hinders our usefulness to God because He wants to use servants who don't embezzle recognition and photobomb His glory.

Remember when God shrunk Gideon's army to a small band of men? God did this so there would be no question whose power saved Israel.

God's goal hasn't changed. He is still putting His glory on display and looking for servants who aren't seeking to be seen. "But this is the one to whom I will look: he who is humble and contrite in spirit and trembles at my word" (Isaiah 66:2). When God looks at my heart, does He find humility? Pride hinders my usefulness in ministry because "God opposes the proud but gives grace to the humble" (1 Peter 5:5).

Only when I stop seeking to be seen can I truly serve God. I need to daily remind myself that everything I am and have is a gift. I don't deserve recognition. If I'm amazed at God, I will be looking at Him, not trying to get others to see me.

It can be a difficult balance in ministry to share what God is doing through the ministry while not drawing attention to ourself. We do need to share the incredible things God is doing, but we also need to guard our hearts against the desire to be seen by others. The temptation can be to take a little glory for ourselves.

Throughout my ministry I have had the goal of making much of God. But I am amazed at the times I've photobombed God by hoping to be seen or recognized for my actions—even just a little. I know in my head that I don't deserve a drop of recognition, but my sinful heart still seeks these words: "Good job, Kyle!" It is okay to appreciate a complement, but if our actions are done for the purpose of the complement or the praise of others, then that is pride.

HOW DO WE REMOVE THE BARRIER OF PRIDE AND GROW IN HUMILITY?

I must daily guard my heart against pride. It is so sneaky that it can even wear a mask of righteousness. Here are a few helpful ways to identify and battle the pride that lurks within, and to grow in humility.

Worship

Daily ask yourself: *Am I lost in awe, or have I lost my awe?* If I have lost my awe, then I need time alone with God to simply worship. I need to be amazed at Him, not me. When we see His greatness, we will see our significance as infinitely less than His. Humility is a right view of God and ourselves in relation to God.

Many people wrongly think that humility grows from an inward focus. They think that if we look at how weak we are, we will become humble. While it's true we are weak, humility grows from a Godward focus, not an inward focus. The starting point is not to look at our inabilities, but at God's abilities. It is not to look at our unworthiness, but to look at God's infinite worthiness. Instead of focusing first on ourselves, our focus needs to be on God. Once we've seen the greatness of God, we will see ourselves correctly.

Humility shouldn't leave us incapacitated by our weakness. This is why humility needs to start with looking at God. Humility starts with an awe of God's power.

"Humble yourselves before the Lord" (James 4:6).

"'Not by might, nor by power, but by my Spirit,' says the Lord of hosts" (Zechariah 4:6).

"I know, O Lord, that the way of man is not in himself, that it is not in man who walks to direct his steps" (Jeremiah 10:23).

"A person cannot receive even one thing unless it is given him from heaven" (John 3:27).

"Now to him who is able to do far more abundantly than all that we ask or think, according to the power at work within us, to him be glory in the church and in Christ Jesus throughout all generations, forever and ever. Amen" (Ephesians 3:20, 21).

Everything that encompasses man—all possessions, wealth, family, appearance, wisdom, and everything in between—comes from God as a gift. It is humbling to know that I am not the source of anything. It is also exceedingly comforting to know that everything I need, even my position in life, will be granted according to His will. While I must labor and work with the ability and strength God supplies, I can rest with peace at the outcome and results. The favor granted in the eyes of others, any fruitfulness of ministry—these are all in the hands of God.

If we start by looking at our own weaknesses, that's where we stay. We will be paralyzed by our inabilities. Rather than focusing on what God is able to do, we will focus on our inability. When we look to God, however, we are awestruck by His ability to work through nobodies, through unworthy servants.

When we look to God, faith is built.

Armed with faith, we leave focused on God, not ourselves. We leave excited about the infinite possibilities of what God can do, not paralyzed by the many things we cannot do. Godly humility leaves us with hearts crying out in faith, "With God all things are possible!" An inward focus is false humility. It leaves us with our heart saying, "With me nothing is possible."

Because of this, true humility is bold and confident. The humble servant is not cowardly. He or she steps out in faith, without fear, because they trust the unstoppable power of God!

Memorize reminders of God's greatness

"Our God is in the heavens; he does all that he pleases" (Psalm 115:3).

Memorize reminders of God's greatness and our weaknesses

"I am the vine; you are the branches. Whoever abides in me and I in him, he it is that bears much fruit, for apart from me you can do nothing" (John 15:5).

"What do you have that you did not receive? If then you received it, why do you boast as if you did not receive it?" (1 Corinthians 4:7)

Ask God to reveal areas of pride

"Search me, O God, and know my heart! Try me and know my thoughts! And see if there be any grievous way in me, and lead me in the way everlasting!" (Psalm 139:23, 24)

Remember that pride robs us of reward

"Beware of practicing your righteousness before other people in order to be seen by them, for then you will have no reward from your Father who is in heaven" (Matthew 6:1).

Always use massive amounts of prayer

Prayer works like poison on pride. If we build everything on the foundation of prayer, it serves as a continual reminder both to us and others that God alone is worthy of glory.

THE BIG PICTURE

Have you been photobombing God or embezzling His glory?

God wants to use servants who don't get in the way of His glory. His ultimate goal is to show His glory. Why would He set His big tasks before servants who are trying to get their own glory? This is why God uses the weak and lowly—because they don't photobomb God! They truly believe in their head and heart that they are nothing apart from God. They gladly step back and allow God to be seen in His full glory. They don't jump in the way!

If we desire to be used by God as a servant after His own heart, we must allow God to remove the barrier of pride within us so we can grow in humility.

Part 4:

THE OASIS - OVERFLOWING TO OTHERS

During the course of my life, God has used the Christlike example of seven men to greatly impact me at different times.

Here are those men: Bob Kennell, when I was in middle school; Kyle Detmers, during high school; Kelly O'Rear, in college; Bob Farison, when I started in ministry; Drew Woods, when learning to raise our children; Don Trott, while preparing for missions; and Bruce McDonald, while on the mission field. These men were a tremendous example, but they also gave of their time. They let me hang out with them. Something about their life drew me and others to spend time with them.

What was it? It wasn't a program or ministry.

It was their life.

The first characteristic each of them shared was this: contagious joy. They loved God, and this was evident on their face and in their life. I loved to be around them because of their joy. Their passion for God spilled into everything they did. They loved the Master more than the ministry. They kept the greatest command to "love the Lord your God with all your heart and with all your soul and with all your mind and with all your strength" (Mark 12:30). As they did, their life was filled to overflowing.

Second, each man also loved others by putting others first. One of the ways they demonstrated this love was through listening. They would actively listen before speaking. After they took in what you were saying, they asked questions. Another way they demonstrated love was by giving of their time. They made time for others and put their needs first. They kept the second greatest command to "love your neighbor as yourself" (Mark 12:31) as their joy and love for God overflowed to others.

Third, all were faithful to share the treasure of God's Word with believers and unbelievers. They were faithful messengers of God's Word. The message flowed from their heart, not simply their head. They were passionate about the message, which caused me and others to love listening to them. The reason they were passionate was because they were sharing from personal experience their relationship with God. It wasn't just head knowledge. The message had so filled their heart that it overflowed in their words.

I and others were drawn to these men because we saw Christ in them. I loved being around them because they radiated Jesus. As Christ filled them, He overflowed from them.

This is what I desire for my life!

I want a life that is filled to overflowing. I want to be like an oasis in the desert to others.

Chapter 11

THE OASIS

Jesus was a friend of sinners. Am I?

"The Son of Man came to seek and to save the lost"
(LUKE 19:10)

WHAT IS THE OASIS?

The life of the true follower of Jesus is like an oasis in a desert. We have the life-giving water of God to share with others. All around us people are dying from thirst. They are lost, but most don't realize it.

This world is a desert. While people may look satisfied, they aren't. The souls of so many are pursuing satisfaction through one avenue or another, but they pursue it through sin, which will never deliver what it promises. In this desert of a world, sin is like a mirage. Just as a mirage tricks the one viewing it into thinking there is something of substance, sin tricks people to think it will satisfy. But when they reach the mirage—when they sin—all they get is a mouthful of sand. There is no life-giving water in sin.

All around us, lost people are running from one mirage to the next. We often see them in the midst of their pursuits, when they are running after the next mirage, so they appear happy at that time. But sin has deceived them into thinking the next mirage is real. At that moment they think they will be satisfied, and our offer of life-giving water may seem unimportant to them.

However, when people realize their pursuit has only been a mirage, this is the time they are most receptive to the gospel. This is when they realize they need living water. If we are connecting to lost people, we can be there to provide life-giving water.

Even when people are in pursuit of the next mirage, God can still break in. We can help them see the pattern of mirage hunting. None of the past mirages have satisfied, and neither will the next. If we are connecting with lost people, we can be in conversations that challenge them to pursue life-giving water, not the mirages of sin.

For us to become an oasis in the desert for searching souls, three things must happen:

1. We must stay connected to God. The only thing we have to offer others is what has flowed through us. We cannot minister from an empty stream.

2. We must allow Him to flow through us and push out the barriers of sin from our life.

3. We must stay connected to lost people. Are we connecting with others to allow God's power to touch their lives? If we are not connected, what's the point of God's power in us?

POOL OR OASIS?

Do you want to be used by God?

God's life-giving water isn't meant for you alone. It isn't meant to be kept to yourself like your own personal pool or private water park. It is meant to be shared.

Christ tells us to "Go therefore and make disciples of all nations" (Matthew 28:19).

How important are someone's last words? Extremely. The person shares what they most want those around them to remember. In Jesus' last words (Matthew 28), He commanded His followers to go and make disciples.

This doesn't mean all of us will go into overseas missions. It does mean we should all be going toward the lost, toward wherever God leads. If God leads us to go to a new land, we must go to the lost day by day in our new land. If God leads us to stay, we must go to the lost each day in our homeland.

To please our master, we must fulfill His last command. To ignore the command to go to the lost and make disciples is like filling a private swimming pool with emergency relief water while, just across the street, people are dying of thirst. Like the unwise servant who buried his talent, we will not please our master if His life-giving water is kept to ourselves and not shared with others.

To reach the lost, we must go and connect. We must go to those who do not have the life-giving water of God and share it with them.

CONNECTING WITH THE LOST

To have the opportunity to share our hope in the gospel, we need to be intentionally building relationships with unbelievers. We need to reach people where they are. The vast majority of people in post-Christian Europe (and, similarly, more and more in the US) are not going to come to church to hear the gospel.

We need to go to them.

In addition to looking for opportunities to share Christ in your everyday interactions with people, we need to find ways to intentionally stay connected to the lost. For many Christians, their circle of unsaved friends is very small. As we grow closer to Christ, it is true that we will have less in common with unbelievers and won't be able to participate in some conversations or activities. However, if our Lord was able to be "a friend of tax collectors and sinners" (Luke 7:34), then so can we.

Sometimes we get so deep in our Christian circles that we might not even know where to go to build friendships with lost people. One of our ABWE (Association of Baptists for World Evangelism) missionaries, Doug Fry, encourages his church members to "find their tribe." In other words, find the people who enjoy doing what you enjoy. Then do your shared interests with these unbelievers. Encourage church members to connect with others by using their interests: running clubs, singing clubs, music groups, gyms, martial arts classes, motorcycle clubs, surfing, CrossFit, hiking, and many more! Find an activity that can be done with unsaved people and connect with them. This is often where gospel conversations happen.

Doug has many examples of how God has used hobbies and interests to connect with the lost. Here's one story he tells:

> "A member of our church introduced me to an unsaved friend. He didn't seem too impressed to learn that I was an 'evangelical pastor,' but when he learned that I was a runner, his ears perked up. We began to talk about running and realized that we had run in some of the same races. One day I discovered that he was signed up for a half-marathon that I was also doing. I looked for him and decided that I would run with him even though he was quite a bit slower than me. After a short time, he began to ask questions about what I did and what evangelicals believed. God gave me a great opportunity to share the gospel with him during the first 40 minutes of the race."

Churches can encourage their people to "find their tribe," equip them to share their faith, and prioritize this in the church schedule. This doesn't mean adding another program. If there are too many church events, members get heavily involved in multiple programs, and their circle of unsaved friends shrinks. Their available time and energy also shrinks. This may mean cutting our church programs or changing the service time to enable church members to have the time and energy to engage the lost.

My goal is to go toward the lost—wherever God has me. No matter where God has me, people must be the priority. It's easy to get our priorities wrong, even in missions, even in ministry. I know from experience that it's easier to prioritize programs and projects instead of people. Jesus always prioritized people. When people are the priority, we will connect with the lost.

Jesus was "a friend of tax collectors and sinners" (Luke 7:34). Are we?

Do we encourage, equip, and give time for our church members to connect with the lost?

FIND YOUR DESERT

To be an oasis for lost souls, we must go to the desert where people need God's life-giving water.

As we look for opportunities to connect with lost people, God may ask us to step out of our comfort zone. He may lead us to connect with a new social club or volunteer somewhere. He may lead us to part-time or full-time ministry. He may lead us into missions. Once we've committed to sharing God's life-giving water with the lost, we must find our desert.

Finding our desert could be as simple as joining a running club or as difficult as going into missions. It may cause us to face life-altering decisions. "Should I go into missions?" "Which ministry?" "Should I change ministries or location?" I wish there was a quick and easy formula to find God's will, but there isn't. It takes a lot of time in prayer.

I have found that if I ask enough questions the path often becomes clear. During our transition from Tanzania to Portugal, I wrote down some basic questions to help me think through the decision. Both options had a list of pros and cons, but I needed to go deeper than that. I needed to examine my heart to make sure I was following God. My tendency is to move toward comfort—the clear and easy path. These questions weren't meant to help me figure out all the details, they were to help me walk by faith even when I didn't know the details. If I know what God has called me to do, I need to step out in faith and trust Him to work out the unknowns. Some questions were touched on previously but are included here because they specifically apply to going to the lost.

QUESTIONS

1. Goal: Do I desire His glory above everything, including my comfort?

Living for God's glory and living for my comfort are usually at odds. When God calls us to "go" it often means leaving behind what is comfortable and stepping into uncertainty. If I love and protect my comfort more than the glory of God, I won't be willing to follow—or stay—as He leads.

When God calls us to follow Him, other loves get in the way. He calls us to stop pursuing money and comfort as our primary aims. The love of money and comfort will hinder us from fully serving God in a way that pleases Him. If He is calling us to go, they will hold us back so we miss the opportunity to be used as a light in the darkness. If He is calling us to give, it will cause us to hold our money so we miss the opportunity to invest our resources. In both cases, we trade eternal reward for temporal reward.

When we were considering moving from South Africa to Tanzania, God tested our love of comfort. He tested us to see if we were willing to give up great friends, ministry, home, car, motorcycle, and pets to follow Him. Was it hard? Absolutely. But pursuing an even greater treasure also made it a joy. Through testing we learn to treasure God Himself more than comfort or the good gifts He gives.

God tested Abraham's love by asking him to give up his son. If God asks you to give up one of His good gifts to live for His glory, will you?

A question kept coming to mind while trying to make this decision: *Should I uproot our family?* As I wrestled with this decision, God encouraged me with this thought: *I am not uprooting our family. I am teaching them where our true roots are. Our true roots are in Christ.* We used the opportunity to teach our children what it means to follow God wherever He leads. By God's grace, our children have risen to the challenge and loved and embraced a more difficult lifestyle.

"So, whether you eat or drink, or whatever you do, do all to the glory of God" (1 Corinthians 10:31).

"And everyone who has left houses or brothers or sisters or father or mother or children or lands, for my name's sake, will receive a hundredfold and will inherit eternal life. But many who are first will be last, and the last first" (Matthew 19:29, 30).

2. Relationship: Am I daily going deeper in my relationship with God?

God wants me to follow Him, not a formula or plan. He wants to work in me before He works through me.

"Now in a great house there are not only vessels of gold and silver but also of wood and clay, some for honorable use, some for dishonorable. Therefore, if anyone cleanses himself from what is dishonorable, he will be a vessel for honorable use, set apart as holy, useful to the master of the house, ready for every good work" (2 Timothy 2:20, 21).

For many years I missed the "if" in these verses. After all, God can use anyone. This is true. But the question is: Do I want to be used as a vessel of gold or clay? Honor or dishonor? If I truly want to be "ready for every good work" I need to be growing in holiness. This growth is an evidence of God's power at work in me. God's power will flow through me to the extent that I allow it to flow *in* me.

Consider an extension cord. The power flows best when there are no shorts, barriers, or breaks in the wire. In my life, sin is like a barrier that resists God's power flowing through me. God first wants to flow through my whole heart and then my hands. My holiness today affects my usefulness tomorrow.

"But this is the one to whom I will look: he who is humble and contrite in spirit and trembles at my word" (Isaiah 66:2).

3. Surrender: Is my answer "yes" before God has ever spoken?

This challenge from my college professor, Kelly O'Rear, has guided me for more than two decades. Most Christians understand this conceptually, but few do in practice. When God lays on our heart an opportunity to serve Him, whether something as simple as sharing the gospel or something as life altering as going into foreign missions, our answer needs to be "yes" before He has ever spoken.

Like a blank job description, will I sign on the dotted line to follow God no matter what? If my answer is not "yes" before God has spoken, then I am trying to stay in control. God wants my surrender, not my approval of His plan.

When our family first began our path toward missions and said yes to a blank job description, I didn't realize how many times I would have to say yes again! Over and over, we must say yes before He has spoken, before we know what lies hidden in the fog of uncertainty. One thing is true: God's path is never easy. But it is always best.

"Not my will, but yours, be done" (Luke 22:42).

4. Need: Do I see a need or a way that God is working around me?

It's easy to formulate a plan of how I'm going to help God or do something for Him. The problem lies in the fact that I don't have the strength to accomplish anything. God is committed to His plan, not mine. If I desire to be used by God, I need to figure out where He is working and join Him.

"Truly, truly, I say to you, the Son can do nothing of his own accord, but only what he sees the Father doing. For whatever the Father does, that the Son does likewise. For the Father loves the Son and shows him all that he himself is doing" (John 5:19, 20).

5. Biblical command: Is there a way in which I need to obey God's Word to meet the need?

Jesus left us with one primary task: to make disciples. Everything we do should be evaluated as to how we are obeying this command. A veteran missionary once said: "There are enough good things to keep us busy twenty-six hours a day. We must devote our attention to the best things." What is the best thing I need to do to see the gospel spread? We all have different roles according to our gifting, but each ministry should be evaluated to see if it is the best use of our time.

At times, the needs can seem overwhelming. When we began the AIDS Care Home, the primary goal was to take the gospel to people who were close to death. We were faced with incredible suffering which led to endless ways to show compassion. It was so easy to be overwhelmed by all the needs. We found that the best way to maintain focus was to keep the gospel first. Each need was run through this filter: would meeting this need help us to show the love of Christ, build relationships, and share the gospel? Meeting needs are not the end goal, they are a means to show Christ and share Christ. "We must devote our attention to the best things."

"So whoever knows the right thing to do and fails to do it, for him it is sin" (James 4:17).

6. Prayer: Have I waited on God in prayer, asking Him to reveal His will, like Jesus did?

It's easy to pray for God to fulfill our plan. It is much harder to pray for His will to be done. This tests our heart to see if we truly desire His glory above our comfort. (See question 1 on this list.)

Retreating to a quiet place with no agenda except to hear from God can be a very revealing experience. When I lay aside my list of desires and say, "Not my will, but yours, be done," God often allows me to see my selfish desires. But I must make time to be still and take this step. It's easy to get bogged down in the details of a decision. Focused prayer forces me to listen to God's voice.

"Father, if you are willing, remove this cup from me. Nevertheless, not my will, but yours, be done" (Luke 22:42).

7. Desire: Is God giving me a growing desire to minister in this way?

God is continually at work in our hearts to grow us into the people He wants us to be and prepare us for the good works He has set in place for us. As God grows our desires to minister to others in a specific way or area, He may be working on our heart to lead us in that direction.

Before God opened the door for me to begin serving as regional director, our family had already begun praying about how we could serve missionaries in a greater way. We had even started looking for opportunities to visit missionaries in other countries in Africa to encourage them. As our desire grew we began praying for an open door to fulfill that desire. God opened a door to fulfill this desire with the regional director role.

"Work out your own salvation with fear and trembling, for it is God who works in you, both to will and to work for his good pleasure" (Philippians 2:12, 13).

8. Courage: Am I facing my problems instead of running away from them?

Far too many decisions are made in reaction to problems (running from something) instead of a response to God's leading (running toward something). It's never a good idea to change ministries if I am running from something. The difficulties I face are God's tools to grow me. Face your problems with courage, Christlikeness, and the strength He provides. Run toward God, not away from problems.

If struggles are interpersonal and you haven't learned to deal with people and problems in one place, they often show up in the next place after you move. Remember, half the problem goes with you everywhere you go: yourself. Make sure changing ministries is the best answer, not just the easy answer.

For dealing with difficult situations: "For I am already being poured out as a drink offering, and the time of my departure has come. I have fought the good fight, I have finished the race, I have kept the faith" (2 Timothy 4:6, 7).

For dealing with difficult people: "If your brother sins against you, go and tell him his fault, between you and him alone. If he listens to you, you have gained your brother. But if he does not listen, take one or two others along with you, that every charge may be established by the evidence of two or three witnesses" (Matthew 18:15, 16).

9. Gifting: Is this in an area of gifting God has given me and my family?

Over the years some ministries have energized me and some have drained me. The reason I love doing ministry that energizes me is because it comes in an area of gifting. This doesn't mean I ignore areas where I am not gifted; it means I ask myself if new opportunities are an area of gifting or weakness. Considering who God has made me to be in the body of Christ helps me find a good ministry fit. No ministry is 100 percent in our area of gifting, but I always try to move toward my gifting rather than away from it.

"Do not neglect the gift you have" (1 Timothy 4:14).

10. Opportunity: Has God opened a door for ministry?

Wait until He does. God often uses providential circumstances to open doors.

I try not to force doors open. It is easy to become impatient and want to speed things up when we are raising support or wanting to launch a new ministry. God constantly reminds me to be patient until He opens the door. Wait for God to work and the opportunity to join Him. Opportunity does not mean easy. The opportunities to join God at work may mean moving across the world, leaving friends, or being involved in a difficult ministry. When God is ready to work, He will open the door.

When we were preparing for missions it took us two years to pay off school debt, then another three and a half years to raise support. I had to learn patience on God's perfect plan. During that time I put these verses on our fridge and memorized them:

> "Remember the former things of old; for I am God, and there is no other; I am God, and there is none like me, declaring the end from the beginning and from ancient times things not yet done, saying, 'My counsel shall stand, and I will accomplish all my purpose,' calling a bird of prey from the east, the man of my counsel from a far country. I have spoken, and I will bring it to pass; I have purposed, and I will do it" (Isaiah 46:9-11).

These verses served as a constant reminder that God would open the door in the day, hour, and minute that was best. He would accomplish His purpose in His time.

> "For a wide door for effective work has opened to me, and there are many adversaries" (1 Corinthians 16:9).

11. Counsel: Have I sought godly counsel (not just "yes men")?

Godly counsel gives us the opportunity to glean from the wisdom of others, to see things from another perspective. Maybe, just maybe, we don't have all the answers and we need the body of Christ to help us see more clearly.

Whenever I've been hesitant to seek godly counsel, it was because I knew deep down that the ministry was probably a bad idea. Forcing myself to always seek counsel on ministry decisions keeps me from moving forward with bad decisions. Either I listen to other's advice or I drop the idea before I share it because I know what my mentors will say!

"In an abundance of counselors there is safety" (Proverbs 11:14).

12. Friend: What would I suggest my best friend do?

Sometimes, if we can simply remove ourselves from the situation and all the emotions that surround our decision, we can see the entire picture more clearly. Asking ourselves how we would advise our friend (or our children) in a similar situation allows us to emotionally distance ourselves and see the big picture of what is best.

When a decision affects us personally, every detail seems equally important. Gaining some distance helps prioritize the vital few variables and allows us to make the best long-term decision. Deep down, we often know the right thing to do if we can just change our perspective. If we know what we should do, will we take our own advice?

"So whoever knows the right thing to do and fails to do it, for him it is sin" (James 4:17).

13. Strategic dependance: Is this beyond my ability so that success fully depends on God's power?

God's ultimate goal in all He does is to put His glory on display. Someone has rightly said: "God loves to show up and show off." Consider this when evaluating ministry decisions. Be willing to step into ministries that are beyond your abilities. We should not be foolish in our decisions, but we should move forward in faith. God will help you know the difference. When we do this, God alone will receive the glory for success.

I'd like to share this story once more, because it fits under this question. When starting the AIDS ministry in South Africa years ago, we were praying about two options: opening a care home or doing home-based care. The care home thrilled me, but also terrified me. How could I raise $150,000 and monthly expenses? I couldn't. If it was up to me, it would be an epic fail. But viewed from the perspective of putting God's power on display, I wanted to move toward greater visible dependence on God so He alone would receive the glory. God is faithful. He provided funding for the care home. He alone deserves the glory! A few years later, when the care home ministry was no longer needed in our area and we switched to training Zulu pastors, we had a building for the ministry. God provided even before we knew the need.

"The Lord said to Gideon, 'The people with you are too many for me to give the Midianites into their hand, lest Israel boast over me, saying, "My own hand has saved me"'" (Judges 7:2).

14. Faith: God asks: Will you trust Me?

This question is a follow-up to number 13. Many times we know which ministry is beyond our ability, but we are hesitant to step out in faith. But God is not asking for our stamp of approval on His strategy. He wants us to trust Him. He wants us to trust that He is strong and wise and able to work everything out in the best way.

When I was considering the AIDS Care Home ministry, I distinctly remember God challenging my heart with this question: *Will you trust Me?* God wanted me to step out in faith into something that would utterly fail if He didn't come through.

"Now to him who is able to do far more abundantly than all that we ask or think, according to the power at work within us, to him be glory in the church and in Christ Jesus throughout all generations, forever and ever. Amen" (Ephesians 3:20, 21).

15. Fear: Will I take the path marked "fear"?

Why does one path feel fearful? Because of what we are view-ing that lies before us. One path looks comfortable, one path looks fearful. But what lies beyond? The path marked "fear" leads to being completely open to whatever the Master calls me to do. It leads to a "Well done, good and faithful servant, enter into the joy of your master!"

When considering the move to East Africa I felt fear know-ing the decision would be hard and require massive change. It would require leaving a home, country, language, friends, and a ministry we loved and starting over. However, my greater fear was reaching the end of my life and have God say to me: "I had so much more I wanted to use you for. If only you had trusted me . . . "

God is going to work, and He will use willing servants. God used Moses, but because of Moses' fear he wasn't God's mouth-piece. I fear missing an opportunity to join what God is doing more than I fear the unknown or loss of comfort.

> "His master said to him, 'Well done, good and faithful ser-vant. You have been faithful over a little; I will set you over much. Enter into the joy of your master'" (Matthew 25:21).

16. Future: 10/10/10/100: Picture your future self.

This question is an adaptation of Suzy Welch's 10/10/10 ques-tion.[14] What is the significance of this decision in ten minutes, ten months, ten years, or one hundred years? How will I feel about the decision at each future point?

Decisions can feel frightening in the moment. There are many unknowns. Even some of the things we do know can be fright-ening. But many times the things we're afraid of are actually very small in relation to the big picture. Like question 15, this one helps you view the decision from a different vantage point.

Thinking about the future significance of completing this book gave me the motivation to finish. I realized that if I were to die without writing this book, I would have missed a big part of what God called me to do. If ten, or one hundred, years from now I was to look back on the decision to write or not write, the choice was extremely clear: write.

"But one thing I do: forgetting what lies behind and straining forward to what lies ahead, I press on toward the goal for the prize of the upward call of God in Christ Jesus" (Philippians 3:13, 14).

17. Step by step: Will I take the first step?

God gives us the next step, not an entire road map. Don't wait for a detailed plan to start following. Just as God called Abraham to "go to the land I will show you," God calls us to follow Him. God often hides the next step until we follow Him in the step He has revealed. We walk one step at a time.

When we were asked to consider the regional director position in East Africa, God gave us a clearly defined ministry to pray about. It was a big step of faith, but we knew where we would be landing. In my mind, it felt like base jumping! God called us to the edge of a cliff and said, "I want you to jump and that is where you will be landing. Trust me."

Our last transition to Western Europe was entirely different. God showed us that we needed to transition, but He didn't show us where to go. Using the base jumping illustration, this move was like standing on top of a mountain in the fog and God saying: "Start running. When you reach the cliff you will fall. When the time is right, you will see where you are landing. Trust me." God is as faithful today as He was in Abraham's day. He still shows us where He wants us to go . . . as we are going. Trust Him.

"Go . . . to the land that I will show you" (Genesis 12:1).

Every day we are called to "go" to the lost. We are called to connect with them so God can overflow from us with His life-giving water!

OVERFLOWING WATERS

The remainder of Part 4 of this book will look at key areas where we overflow when connecting with others: Overflowing Joy, Overflowing Love, and Overflowing Message. Without these areas, our waters will not be sweet. They will be bitter.

When the children of Israel came to the bitter waters of Marah, even though they were desperate for water, they cried out, "What shall we drink?" (Exodus 15:24). The taste repelled them! If our waters are not sweet, we are like bitter waters in the desert; we will repel people rather than draw them. Our message may be sound, but if it is not overflowing with joy and love, it will not be sweet.

Why are waters bitter? Usually because they are stagnant. There is little flowing in and little flowing out. If we don't connect with others, we grow stagnant and bitter. We become like the waters of Marah instead of an oasis. If we want sweet waters, we must have much of Christ flowing into us and overflowing to others.

Let's take the path together that will move us toward becoming an oasis!

Chapter 12

OVERFLOWING JOY

Does my life radiate joy in the Lord . . . always?

"Rejoice in the Lord always; again I will say, rejoice"
(PHILIPPIANS 4:4).

WHAT IS JOY?

Joy is a response to seeing or obtaining that which we value. It is impossible to pursue joy itself. We must pursue joy in something. John Piper says, "Christian joy is a good feeling in the soul, produced by the Holy Spirit, as he causes us to see the beauty of Christ in the word and in the world."[15]

WHY DOES JOY MATTER TO US?

1. Joy is necessary to please God.

If I want my service to please God, I must obey all His commands, which means my service must be done in joy. If I want my giving to please the Lord, it must come from an overflow of joy in God. My service and giving should not be done "reluctantly or under compulsion, for God loves a cheerful giver" (2 Corinthians 9:7). I cannot separate joy from service. Joy is evidence that my heart is engaged in the service, not just my mind. The presence of joy means God is flowing through my whole heart and changing my inner man, not just my outer deeds.

It's possible to serve in a way that doesn't please God! Psalms 37:4 commands us to "Delight yourself in the Lord, and he will give you the desires of your heart." Enjoying God is a command. Therefore, if we are not finding our joy in God, we are walking in disobedience.

If our delight is in God, what will the desires of our heart be? More of God, not a new car or house. Seeing more of God Himself is what will satisfy and delight our heart. If we search with the right heart, God promises to give us more of Himself. "You will seek the Lord your God and you will find him, if you search after him with all your heart and with all your soul" (Deuteronomy 4:29).

2. Joy is important because, if we are not finding our joy in God, we are seeking it elsewhere.

We are always seeking joy in something. If we are not finding our joy in God, we are looking for it somewhere else. When this happens we are treasuring something else as more valuable or satisfying than God!

Our problem is we are too easily pleased with lesser things. C.S. Lewis put this well.

> "If there lurks in most modern minds the notion that to desire our own good and earnestly to hope for the enjoyment of it is a bad thing, I submit that this notion has crept in from Kant and the Stoics and is no part of the Christian faith. Indeed, if we consider the unblushing promises of reward and the staggering nature of the rewards prom-

ised in the Gospels, it would seem that our Lord finds our desires not too strong, but too weak. We are half-hearted creatures fooling about with drink and sex and ambition when infinite joy is offered us, like an ignorant child who wants to go on making mud pies in a slum because he cannot imagine what is meant by the offer of a holiday at the sea. We are far too easily pleased."[16]

We must pursue that which brings us the greatest delight, namely God Himself. May our hearts long for, seek after, be satisfied in, and worship God as David did.

"O God, you are my God; earnestly I seek you; my soul thirsts for you; my flesh faints for you, as in a dry and weary land where there is no water. So I have looked upon you in the sanctuary, beholding your power and glory. Because your steadfast love is better than life, my lips will praise you. So I will bless you as long as I live; in your name I will lift up my hands. My soul will be satisfied as with fat and rich food, and my mouth will praise you with joyful lips" (Psalm 63:1-5).

3. Joy is important because it is connected to our strength.

When my focus stays on God, joy is the result. When I lack energy and strength in ministry, it is usually because my focus has moved off the Lord. Nehemiah reminded the Israelites of this connection when he said, "The joy of the LORD is your strength" (Nehemiah 8:10). If I lose my joy in God, my strength and energy fade away.

When I am finding joy in God I will delight in His plan, provision, and promises. I will be satisfied, content, and at peace. Joy has far more to do with what we focus on than on our circumstances. Focusing on God fills us with joy because He is the object of our joy. It fills us with hope because He is in control of all events. It fills us with strength because He is always with us.

When my focus shifts off God, joy vanishes. A few warning signs that I am not finding my joy in God are worry, complaining, and sarcasm. When I notice these things, it is a reminder to refocus on God. Worry is when I am not *confident* in God's plan. Complaining and sarcasm are when I am not *happy* with God's plan. They all focus on the negative and destroy joy for me, my family, and the teams I serve. Joy is like oxygen for strength. Without joy, strength dies. Strength suffocates when the air that surrounds my life is filled with worry, complaining, or negative sarcasm.

If I lack strength and energy in ministry I must ask myself, have I lost "the joy of the Lord"?

WHY DOES JOY MATTER TO GOD?

Imagine a servant who obeys the king's commands and tells others to do the same, but has no joy in doing so. He also finds no joy in personally praising the king. The servant obeys out of duty alone, not from joy.

A joyless servant would not honor his king. When other people see a joyless servant they will want to avoid the king, not serve the king. When the king sends an ambassador, he wants to send someone who finds joy in him and serving him.

"God is most glorified in us when we are most satisfied in Him." — John Piper[17]

Jonathan Edwards wrote: "God is glorified not only by His glory's being seen, but by its being rejoiced in. When those that see it delight in it, God is more glorified than if they only see it."[18]

We glorify God best when we delight in Him. Why?

Reason 1: God is more glorified when we delight in who He is because it results in us joyfully displaying His glory.

Psalm 32:11 says, "Be glad in the Lord, and rejoice, O righteous, and shout for joy, all you upright in heart!"

Psalm 40:16: "May all who seek you rejoice and be glad in you; may those who love your salvation say continually, 'Great is the Lord!'"

Both verses have a two-step pattern: First to be glad and rejoice in God, and second to joyfully display His glory. The God-given natural response of the human heart is to praise the things that bring satisfaction and delight in our lives.

Psalm 16:11 says, "In Thy presence is fullness of joy." What happens when you continue to pour into a cup after it's full? It overflows. The same thing happens when we experience fullness of joy. Fullness of joy is much more than just feeling happy. It's being so full of joy that we are unable to keep it to ourselves because it overflows from our life. God glorifies Himself by fully satisfying us with Himself, because then our delight overflows into joyfully proclaiming His glory.

Unbelievers are desperately seeking satisfaction and enjoyment in life. They seek it anywhere they can. If I am not joyfully satisfied in God, I will not be an effective witness for Him. Why would unbelievers listen to my words if I am just as unsatisfied as they are? They won't listen if they don't see a difference in my life. My enjoyment of God needs to be real. If it's fake, they'll see right through it.

We must be filled with enjoyment and delight in God so that these things will overflow continually from our lives.

Reason 2: God is more glorified when we delight in who He is than if we are unaffected by Him.

"This people honors me with their lips, but their heart is far from me; in vain do they worship me" (Matthew 15:8, 9).

Consider this illustration about an interaction between a husband and wife on Valentine's Day. Which of these two statements would glorify the wife more?

1. "Because I am your husband, it is my duty to take you out to dinner this Valentine's Day." This attitude would crush any wife. Why? It belittles her worth because her husband is acting out of a joyless sense of duty. He does not enjoy her for who she is.

2. "Because I love you and enjoy being with you so much, it would be my pleasure to take you out to dinner this Valentine's Day." This attitude would thrill any wife. Why? It shows that her husband enjoys her and loves being with her. She knows she is valuable to him because he enjoys her simply for who she is.

What if these same attitudes carried over in our relationship with God? Which of the next two statements would glorify God?

1. "Lord, I will spend time with you and tell others about you because it is my duty." This attitude does not glorify God. It belittles God's worth when actions are done out of a joyless sense of duty. Doing things out of duty is not always wrong. But duty must be done with the right attitude. The great sin of the Pharisees was they were obeying God only from duty, but their heart was far from God.

2. "Lord, because I love and enjoy you so much, I want to spend time with you and tell others about you." This attitude glorifies God because it shows He is valued in our life. The attitude behind our actions is just as important as the action itself. When we enjoy God above all else, including His gifts, we show the world that He fully satisfies us.

If we do not enjoy God, we belittle His worth.

Reason 3: Our body language is always communicating.

Our body language communicates joy. Even when we are not speaking, we are communicating! Whether we like it or not, our body language always shows what's in our heart. When we have joy, it overflows to our face and body. Our smile shows it. Not the fake kind that you plaster on, but a true smile that engages the eyes.

A true smile on the face overflows from a truly joyful heart. Joy honors the *object* of our joy and says it is satisfied with that object. In a world where people long to be satisfied, our joyful countenance honors God.

HOW CAN WE GROW IN JOY?

Remember that joy is a response to seeing or obtaining that which we value. It is impossible to pursue joy itself; we must pursue joy *in something*. To grow in joy we must pursue that which will bring us joy. We must meditate on our object of joy. That which fills our thoughts is in our mind's eye. To delight in these things, we must "think about these things" (Philippians 4:8).

What will bring us joy? What should we be filling our mind with and thinking about?

1. Joy in God Himself

Moses' request to God has become my daily prayer as I open God's Word or meditate on it: "Show me your glory" (Exodus 33:18). This prayer flows from the realization that seeing more of God's glory will satisfy my soul more than anything else in the world. The more deeply I know Him, the more deeply I will delight in Him. He is my soul's treasure!

"Rejoice *in the Lord* always; again I will say, rejoice" (Philippians 4:4).

"*In your presence* there is fullness of joy" (Psalm 16:11).

God is the object of our joy!

2. Joy in seeing God glorified

Because we delight in God, we also delight in the manifestation of His glory. We love to see God glorified, and this is the reason behind our every action. "So, whether you eat or drink, or whatever you do, do all to the glory of God" (1 Corinthians 10:31). We delight to see His glory.

There is a subtle yet dangerous mutation of this joy. We must beware of switching from joy in seeing God glorified to joy in ministry success. I have fallen prey to this before, and it was so subtle that I missed it for years.

Here's how it works. We begin pursuing ministry with a passion to see God glorified, but at this point there is no specific ministry. We pray that God would glorify Himself through us. As God clarifies our direction and opens doors, we get involved in a specific ministry and begin praying that God will glorify Himself through this ministry. So far, so good.

Here's where the mutation happens. We begin to see our ministry success as synonymous with God's glory, but it isn't. We think that the primary way God is going to use us for His glory is by having our ministry plans succeed. God may have an entirely different plan which might involve our plans failing. God may use our failed plans to open a new door. He may use our response to failure as a testimony that brings people to faith. Our ministry may be a failure by our standards, but God can still be getting the glory He desires.

When we were operating the care home for AIDS patients, I longed for God to be glorified, but I let the success of my ministry begin to be synonymous with God's glory. I began to delight in and long for ministry success instead of longing for God's glory to be seen. I didn't realize this had happened until after we had closed the care home.

Even if our ministry plans never "succeed" according to our desires, will we be joyful if God's glory is seen?

When Paul's ministry was not going well by human standards because he was in chains and others were causing trouble for him, where did he find joy? "Only that in every way, whether in pretense or in truth, Christ is proclaimed, and in that I rejoice" (Philippians 1:18). Paul's joy, and ours, was and is found in Christ being proclaimed and God being glorified.

3. Joy in our future in Heaven

"Nevertheless, do not rejoice in this, that the spirits are subject to you, but rejoice that your names are written in heaven" (Luke 10:20).

No matter what happens, this joy should not be shaken because this hope cannot be taken. Jesus reminded His disciples that joy in our future hope should surpass our joy in ministry success! Success may come and go, but our joy in Heaven should cause an unshakable joy.

We should have an unshakable joy because we have an unshakable future!

Ministry and missions require sacrifice. You will have to let some things go. But even in the loss, God promises to reward. He gives us what we need in this life and rewards us in the next. "And everyone who has left houses or brothers or sisters or father or mother or children or lands, for my name's sake, will receive a hundredfold and will inherit eternal life. But many who are first will be last, and the last first" (Matthew 19:29, 30). This promise is vital to persevering in ministry! God often blesses us even in this life, and we should be wise with our finances, but money and possessions shouldn't be our pursuit. Whenever the idea of a high-paying job, owning a house, being closer to family, or more stability tries to lure me away from ministry, this promise reminds me of my future joy. I need to stay in the center of His will day by day. I can't let other things get in the way of following God wherever He leads. To do so would be to exchange my future reward for lesser joys.

Even if God calls you to stay, it requires sacrifice. He calls us to serve and give sacrificially. The loss is different, but as we give back what God has given us, He promises to reward us. "Lay up for yourselves treasures in heaven" (Matthew 6:20).

Like compounded interest on an eternal scale, we lay possessions, opportunities, and relationships at His feet and He will return them with compounded interest in Heaven.

4. Joy in walking according to God's design

There is great joy in walking in obedience to God. We were made to live in fellowship with Him. As we walk with Him, He abides in us (John 15), and in His presence is fullness of joy!

"For I find my delight in your commandments, which I love. I will lift up my hands toward your commandments, which I love, and I will meditate on your statutes" (Psalms 119:47, 48).

"The law of your mouth is better to me than thousands of gold and silver pieces" (Psalms 119:72).

"Your word is a lamp to my feet and a light to my path" (Psalms 119:105).

"Your commandments are my delight" (Psalms 119:143).

Joy is an outward evidence. It's a fruit of walking by faith, the result of living according to God's plan for our life. As seen in Part

3 of this book, holiness and walking according to God's design also makes us useful to God for service, and we will find great joy in being useful to our master.

We were created to glorify God. As He works through us to glorify Himself we find great joy in living according to God's design.

5. Joy in seeing sinners come to faith

"I tell you, there is joy before the angels of God over one sinner who repents" (Luke 15:10).

One of the great joys in ministry is when the spiritually lost are found, when the spiritually blind see, when the spiritually dead are raised to life to become children of God. When AIDS patients in South Africa came to faith in Christ it was amazing to see their joy. Their entire countenance changed as their fear was replaced with joy and peace.

We love to see others begin to treasure what we treasure. Think about what we most naturally do with anything we enjoy. We love to see others enjoy it also! We love to share our joy with them so we can partake in joy together. The greatest joy we have to share is the joy of salvation.

6. Joy in God's sovereignty (God's perfect plan and power)

One of the clearest times when we put God's glory on display is when we deal with problems and trials.

It's like we are under a giant spotlight and others are watching to see how we respond. How we respond is showing others—really, teaching others—who God is. If we respond well to trials it shows others that God is dependable and can be trusted.

As we go through trials, others are watching. They are watching to see if we respond in faith.

Having peace in the midst of comfort is normal. Having peace in the midst of trials is not normal. Trials give us an opportunity to demonstrate the peace and hope we have. If we complain, get sarcastic, or have a bad attitude when facing trials, we forfeit the opportunity to speak of the greatness of God!

God entrusts us with trials so we can be a light. Let's not waste these opportunities.

"But even if you should suffer for righteousness' sake, you will be blessed. Have no fear of them, nor be troubled, but in your hearts honor Christ the Lord as holy, always being prepared to make a defense to anyone who asks you for a reason for the hope that is in you" (1 Peter 3:14, 15).

If we respond well to trials, not only does it show He is trustworthy, it also shows others He is infinitely valuable. Our joy won't be based on circumstances or comfort, but on the unchangeable nature of God Himself. When people interact with us, they will see our joy in Christ, and we will be like an oasis in their lives.

THE BIG PICTURE

We can only give to others what is flowing through us. We cannot minister from an empty stream. We need to be connected to the source, the spring of life, by taking time to worship Him. We need to remove the boulders and hindrances of sin that are blocking God flowing freely through us. We also need to make sure we are not fighting against God by pursuing personal recognition instead of His glory alone.

We can be an oasis in the desert to share God with others. God is what everyone's soul longs for, and it is the only thing that will satisfy.

Our joy in God will flow through our life of love and message of hope.

Chapter 13

OVERFLOWING LOVE

Do I love God by loving others?

"And this commandment we have from him:
whoever loves God must also love his brother"
(1 JOHN 4:21).

WHAT IS LOVE?

Love is the sacrificial giving of ourselves, putting the needs of others before our own, putting their good before our good.

"Love is patient and kind; love does not envy or boast; it is not arrogant or rude. It does not insist on its own way; it is not irritable or resentful; it does not rejoice at wrongdoing, but rejoices with the truth. Love bears all things, believes all things, hopes all things, endures all things" (1 Corinthians 13:4-7).

Let's break it down further.

1. God is love and love begins with God.

"Love is from God" (1 John 4:7). God demonstrated what love is by giving us His love. To see love defined, we look to God. His actions embody love.

> "Beloved, let us love one another, for love is from God, and whoever loves has been born of God and knows God. Anyone who does not love does not know God, because God is love. In this the love of God was made manifest among us, that God sent his only Son into the world, so that we might live through him" (1 John 4:7-9).

God is the starting point for love. My ability to truly love others depends on God dwelling in me and my relationship with Him. If I have a love problem with others, I have a love problem with God.

2. Love is not dependent on the recipient. It is dependent on the giver.

"In this is love, not that we have loved God but that he loved us and sent his Son to be the propitiation for our sins" (1 John 4:10).

This truth has deeply impacted me. Love can begin even if only one side chooses to love. God chose to love us even when we were His enemies and running from Him. The giver of love sets the terms. If the giver chooses to love unconditionally, then the love doesn't change because there is not a condition that can change it. There's no kill switch. This can be hard to remember when we are tired, stressed, or discouraged, but love depends on a choice, not circumstances. The choice to love is one we face day by day. Don't let circumstances be an excuse not to love. Love depends on you, not the recipient.

3. Our love toward others is dependent on our love to God.

"We love because he first loved us. If anyone says, 'I love God,' and hates his brother, he is a liar; for he who does not love his brother whom he has seen cannot love God whom he has not seen. And this commandment we have from him: whoever loves God must also love his brother" (1 John 4:19-21).

If our hearts truly love God, our actions will prove it. Loving others is the test. It puts what's in our hearts on display for others to see.

If we are unloving, it should be like a warning bell that we're not loving God as we should. This includes not only unloving words, but everything that flows from our heart, including unloving body language (rolling the eyes, making a face) and the tone of our voice (sarcastic, irritated, and more).

WHY DOES LOVE MATTER TO US?

1. It is necessary to please God.

It is possible to serve in a way that doesn't please God. If we want our service to please God, it must be marked by love. Consider these passages that put love as central to pleasing God.

"'I am the Lord who practices steadfast love, justice, and righteousness in the earth. For in these things I delight,' declares the Lord" (Jeremiah 9:24).

"He has told you, O man, what is good; and what does the Lord require of you but to do justice, and to love kindness, and to walk humbly with your God" (Micah 6:8).

"And you shall love the Lord your God with all your heart and with all your soul and with all your mind and with all your strength. The second is this: You shall love your neighbor as yourself. There is no other commandment greater than these" (Mark 12:30, 31).

"If anyone says, 'I love God,' and hates his brother, he is a liar; for he who does not love his brother whom he has seen cannot love God whom he has not seen" (1 John 4:20).

When we serve without love, we serve while breaking God's command. How will our service please God if we are going against His clear instructions? To please God we must live in the way He commands.

2. Serving without love does not benefit us in the end.

"If I speak in the tongues of men and of angels, but have not love, I am a noisy gong or a clanging cymbal. And if I have prophetic powers, and understand all mysteries and all knowledge, and if I have all faith, so as to remove mountains, but have not love, I am nothing. If I give away all I have, and if I deliver up my body to be burned, but have not love, I gain nothing" (1 Corinthians 13:1-3).

Serving without love gains us nothing! Without love we will be serving in vain.

But is it OK to love others for our own gain? 1 Corinthians 13:5 says that "love does not seek its own." If we are seeking our own reward, isn't that seeking our own?

When Paul says that love does not seek its own, he is saying that love does not seek its own and exclude seeking the good of others. Love toward others means meeting their current needs above our current needs. Love seeks to meet the existing needs of others, and by doing so this benefits our eternal reward.

3. Love is necessary for God to spiritually bless our ministry.

When we love others, God Himself fills our life. The apostle John said, "Whoever abides in love abides in God, and God abides in him" (1 John 4:16). Remember back to the example of two objects not being able to fill the same space. When we are loving ourselves instead of others and God, we are filling the space. We are on the throne of our heart because we are loving ourselves. When we climb off the throne and allow God to take that spot, He will fill us with Himself.

If we are not abiding in God, we are operating in our own strength, and we will bear no spiritual fruit. How sad that so much "ministry" is done in the power of the flesh, without the power of God, because we, as servants, are not abiding in God. If we want God to work through us, the priority of our life must be to abide in Him. No spiritual fruit is produced when we minister in our own strength.

This may seem simple, but it is frightening how many times we try to minister to others but are not walking in love toward others. We can make the formula pretty simple.

No love = no abiding = no fruit.

Love = abiding = fruit.

Our love toward others is essential if we desire God to spiritually bless our lives and ministry.

WHY DOES LOVE MATTER TO GOD?

We've used this word-picture before, and though it is simple, it's important. So let's return to it: Imagine a servant who tells others how loving and kind the king is. No one had ever seen a truly loving person, so the servant's explanation of love as being patient and kind was their only understanding of love. But then the servant turns around and is impatient, unkind, and unloving toward his family and others. The servant said love was one thing, but he didn't demonstrate it. Would this servant honor the king? No. The servant's life did not help people to see the king's love. The people needed to see an example of love.

On an even deeper level, a lack of love for others shows that he loves himself more than the king. If the servant truly loved the king, he would show it by loving others.

A servant who loves himself more than the king is not a true servant. This servant is using his role as a servant to serve himself. He may be offering some service to the king, but it is not wholehearted. The servant thinks he is more important than the king. After all, the servant is listening to his own desires, not the king's. The servant is placing himself on the throne when he loves himself rather than loving others.

When we love others, it allows them to see God.

God's ultimate goal is to have His glory clearly seen. If "God is love," then He wants others to have a clear example of Himself lived out through us (1 John 4:8). Others can't see God with their eyes, but as they watch us they see what God's love is like.

"No one has ever seen God; if we love one another, God abides in us and his love is perfected in us" (1 John 4:12).

As we love we put God on display for others to see. They see what love truly is. As we sacrificially give of ourselves, others can understand the nature of God's love, of One who gave of Himself to die for our sins and make a way of salvation.

This means how we love our spouse, children, coworkers, church, friends, neighbors, and world is extremely important. Our love (or lack thereof) is always speaking! With far more weight than any sermon or message, your love and kindness is a moment-by-moment message of what God is like! Our love validates our words. If our life is unloving, our words will be unheeded.

Our love matters to God.

HOW DO WE GROW IN LOVE?

1. We show our love toward God by loving others.

"And you shall love the Lord your God with all your heart and with all your soul and with all your mind and with all your strength. The second is this: You shall love your neighbor as yourself. There is no other commandment greater than these" (Mark 12:30, 31). If we truly love God with all our heart, soul, mind, and strength, how do we show it? By loving others. "We love because he first loved us. If anyone says, 'I love God,' and hates his brother, he is a liar; for he who does not love his brother whom he has seen cannot love God whom he has not seen. And this commandment we have from him: whoever loves God must also love his brother" (1 John 4:19-21).

As we love God, we serve Him instead of ourselves. The way that we serve God is by loving others. God is not right in front of us. He's in Heaven. The practical way we show our love to God is by loving those around us. We love God through loving others.

It's not that we love others because they are lovely. There was nothing lovely in us that caused God to love us. We were His enemies! We are called to love God, who is lovely. The way we act out that love for God is by loving others. As we do this, others see an example of what God's love is.

Picture those you are called to love standing between you and God. The way your love gets to God is through them. Our attitude toward others is a reflection of our attitude toward God.

Do I love God by loving others?

2. We follow His example.

"So if there is any encouragement in Christ, any comfort from love, any participation in the Spirit, any affection and sympathy, complete my joy by being of the same mind, having the same love, being in full accord and of one mind. Do nothing from selfish ambition or conceit, but in humility count others more significant than yourselves. Let each of you look not only to his own interests, but also to the interests of others. *Have this mind among yourselves, which is yours in Christ Jesus,* who, though he was in the form of God, did not count equality with God a thing to be grasped, but emptied himself, by taking the form of a servant, being born in the likeness of men. And being found in human form, he humbled himself by becoming obedient to the point of death, even death on a cross" (Philippians 2:1-8).

As we look at the example of Christ's love, we will see areas of our life where we are not acting in love.

Christ's life defines love. As we look at His life, we know how we should live. How did Christ love? He counted others as more significant and looked out for their interests.

How far did He go? He gave His very life. When we are tempted to hold onto our life, time, or possessions, let's remember the love of Christ is our example!

Do I love others as Christ has loved me?

3. We hold our life, time, and possessions with an open hand.

Everything we have is a gift from God. "What do you have that you did not receive?" (1 Corinthians 4:7) When we learn to see everything as a gift, and not as something we earned, we can more freely share ourselves and our possessions. David recognized that he was simply taking from the Lord's hand and giving back to Him. "But who am I, and what is my people, that we should be able thus to offer willingly? For all things come from you, and of your own have we given you" (1 Chronicles 29:14).

Everything we have is for investment purposes. "And he who had received the five talents came forward, bringing five talents more, saying, 'Master, you delivered to me five talents; here, I have made five talents more.' His master said to him, 'Well done, good and faithful servant. You have been faithful over a little; I will set you over much. Enter into the joy of your master'" (Matthew 25:21). When our life, time, and possessions are seen as opportunities to invest in future reward and future joy, we hold them with an open hand.

If God calls us to give our life to full-time ministry, our time when it is inconvenient, or our possessions, it tests what we love. If God calls us to go and leave family to serve overseas, it will test our love of family, comfort, and possessions. If God calls us to serve others with our time, it will test whether we hold tightly to our time or whether we will give it away. If God calls us to give to others or give up something to follow Him, it tests our love of things.

I remember when we were praying about moving from South Africa to Tanzania. I knew I couldn't take my motorcycle. God tested my love to see if I would put that gift back into His hand. What was my greater love? Would I hold my possessions with an open hand? We and our kids would have to leave a home, foods, language, friends, and pets we loved. Would we trust Him to provide what was best in a new location?

If you hold your life, time, and possessions with an open hand, it hurts much less when God calls you to give these things back to Him. Giving back to God is a test of our love.

Do I hold my life, time, and possessions with an open hand?

4. We store up treasure in Heaven.

"Do not lay up for yourselves treasures on earth, where moth and rust destroy and where thieves break in and steal, but lay up for yourselves treasures in heaven, where neither moth nor rust destroys and where thieves do not break in and steal. For where your treasure is, there your heart will be also" (Matthew 6:19-21).

What is our treasure? If our hearts are linked to earth, it's because earth is where we have stored all of our treasures! If we are treasuring all this world has to offer, we will hoard our time and resources for ourselves—we won't lovingly give them away.

In order for us to show love to others by freely giving of our life, time, and possessions, our greatest treasure needs to be in Heaven. We must go after treasure that will last, and that means loving others.

Am I treasuring my life, my time, and my possessions, or will I give those away and treasure heavenly reward?

EVALUATING OUR HEART AND LIFE

It's easy to think that if life was easier I wouldn't get impatient, frustrated, or angry. When I begin thinking this way I long for comfort and lack of problems. But whenever I am frustrated or unloving, the events or people aren't the real problem. The people or events are simply God's tool to reveal my heart. Like fire placed under gold to heat it and refine the impurities when they rise to the surface, God uses difficult circumstances to refine my heart. When I face a difficult situation and become unloving, it reveals my heart. It allows me to see that I am not as patient or loving as I imagined.

I repeat this next passage because it is so critically important: "Love is patient and kind; love does not envy or boast; it is not arrogant or rude. It does not insist on its own way; it is not irritable or resentful; it does not rejoice at wrongdoing, but rejoices with the truth. Love bears all things, believes all things, hopes all things, endures all things" (1 Corinthians 13:4-7).

If I am acting in impatience, unkindness, boasting, arrogance, rudeness, insisting on my own way, irritation, or resentment . . . these are all indications of an unloving heart!

Over the years, God has challenged me with a few questions to evaluate my heart and life. These questions help me detect an unloving heart. By identifying an unloving heart and the actions that accompany it, I can seek God's help to grow and change. Like a doctor looks for the early warning signs of cancer, these are warning signs that an unloving heart is taking root in my life. The sooner I deal with it the better.

1. Is pride affecting my love?

Pride is often the root of my unloving attitude. When I get frustrated with others for their actions, what I'm really saying is this: "I would never do anything like *that*, so I am justified at being frustrated and unloving toward you!" This can apply to many areas of life—when others are forgetful, late, drive poorly, are inefficient at their job, and more. When I get frustrated with others, it is really my pride congratulating myself that I am not like them. It is my pride saying, "You are better than that person. You have every right to be frustrated and unloving with them!" John MacArthur said that our "anger is connected to self-worship."[19] Pride is lifting up myself by looking down on others.

> "Do nothing from selfish ambition or conceit, but in humility count others more significant than yourselves" (Philippians 2:3).

2. Do I love others by giving them the same grace I give myself?

When someone does something that frustrates me, irritates me, messes up my plan, causes more work, or breaks my schedule . . . well, in truth, my perspective is often self-centered. I think about how the other person's actions affect *me*. When I am the center of my universe, I feel justified in being frustrated or unloving because of the other person's actions. I may even think they did something to intentionally frustrate me.

Most people are not intentionally doing things to irritate or bother me. Like me many times, they act as if the world revolves around them. They do what they think is best to maintain their comfort, *the same thing I try to do.* The book *How to Win Friends and Influence People* encourages us to, "Stop a minute to contrast your keen interest in your own affairs with your mild concerns about anything else. Realize, then, that everybody else in the world feels exactly the same way! Then . . . you will have grasped the only solid foundation for interpersonal relationships; namely, that success in dealing with people depends on a sympathetic grasp of the other person's viewpoint."[20]

What story do I tell myself if I need to cut in traffic? I justify it because I am running late or because I didn't see my exit. Do I ever call myself a jerk? Nope. I give myself grace because I tell myself a different story. *There's a reason I needed to cut,* I say. When I get upset at others and am unloving, I'm not considering their story. I only have my perspective and the facts I know— or think I know. What if they are rushing to the hospital for an emergency? What if they didn't see their exit? After getting more information, my attitude totally changes when I understand the full story.

When frustration starts to rise I now ask myself: Could there be another side to the story that would make this situation understandable from the other person's perspective? Is it possible they may have had a problem that caused them to leave late? Sometimes I cut the line in traffic when running late! I don't pick up after myself 100 percent of the time! Everyone has a reason and a story. I use the suggestion from *Crucial Accountability*— "Ask why a reasonable, rational, and decent person would do what you've just seen."[21] Do I give others the same grace I give myself?

"So whatever you wish that others would do to you, do also to them" (Matthew 7:12).

3. Am I being changed by difficulties or controlled by them?

We covered trials in the chapter on faith, but trials and problems also affect our love. Am I being controlled by events and circumstances, or by truth? Is my attitude being determined by other's actions and circumstances, or by the love of Christ? "For the love of Christ controls us, because we have concluded this: that one has died for all, therefore all have died; and he died for all, that those who live might no longer live for themselves but for him who for their sake died and was raised" (2 Corinthians 5:14, 15).

When I let people's actions cause frustration, anger, or an unloving attitude, I am allowing their actions to determine whether I have a good or bad day. Not only does it affect my mood, it could even affect my life span since many health problems are stress-induced. Instead, I must be controlled and guided by truth and the Spirit, not the actions of others. Galatians 5:18-23 is a great passage to study in this regard.

Frustrations are like God's gym. They make us stronger. Without physical exercise I will stay weak. Without more strenuous exercise I will never grow stronger. I need more resistance. In the same way, God allows difficulties or difficult people to make me stronger by stretching me to love others.

Difficulties also strengthen and prepare me for greater ministry challenges so I can be a testimony in all circumstances. Before God gives me greater opportunities, He gives me smaller ones. Traffic jams, plans that fail, flight delays, and more. How do

I handle these small tests? If I get frustrated with little things and act in an unloving way, why would God give me ministry opportunities where I could publicly make Him look small and not in control by my frustration? Remember Moses when he responded in frustration to the people of Israel? God takes our reactions seriously because it reflects on His character. God wants me to respond in love.

> "Count it all joy, my brothers, when you meet trials of various kinds, for you know that the testing of your faith produces steadfastness. And let steadfastness have its full effect, that you may be perfect and complete, lacking in nothing" (James 1:2-4).

4. Am I dealing with little frustrations in a loving way?

Do I get frustrated, angry, or unloving over little things? Even the little things need to be dealt with. As Solomon said, it is "the little foxes that spoil the vineyards" (Song of Solomon 2:15). Small unloving acts and attitudes are still sin.

What's in our heart will come out. Sin is like lava in our heart that wants to erupt. Trying to avoid eruptions of sin without dealing with the lava in our heart is like trying to cap a volcano. If you cap the top it will vent out the side. Even if we don't have angry outbursts or fits of rage, if we are impatient or unkind it reveals our heart. The unloving heart will vent in a different direction. Little frustrations reveal our bigger heart problems.

Amy Carmichael once said, "A cup brimful of sweetness cannot spill even one drop of bitter water, no matter how suddenly jarred."[22] When I am unloving and that is what comes out, it is just my heart being revealed. As one of my professors used to say, "You can fake your actions, not your reactions." My reactions are a more accurate reflection of my heart because they are rarely filtered or polished. My reactions reveal if I am walking in the Spirit.

If my heart is ruled by Christ, peace and love come out. If my heart is ruled by anger and frustration, anger comes out. When I am jarred, what comes out of my heart? I need to deal with all manifestations of an unloving heart, both big and small.

"And let the peace of Christ rule in your hearts, to which indeed you were called in one body. And be thankful" (Colossians 3:15).

5. Am I creating margin so I can be patient and loving to others?

I set myself up for failure and frustration when I don't schedule margin into my life. This sets me up to respond in unloving ways. Most of us try to stack events in our day with the efficiency of an air traffic controller: one commitment right after the other. The problem is we don't know what unplanned events God has planned.

With no margin, we are headed for stress now or a stroke later. It's just smart advice: expect the unexpected.

This is an area in which I am trying to improve. I used to cause my family unnecessary stress by not leaving enough margin in my schedule. The book *Essentialism* suggests adding "50 percent to your time estimate."[23] Now, if I think it will take ten minutes to get to the store, I want to plan to leave fifteen minutes early. If I think it will take thirty minutes to get ready, I plan for forty-five. This allows me to stay relaxed when the unexpected happens. If I arrive or finish early, it allows me to slow down and enjoy God, family, friends, and life. It allows me to have time to love others and help meet their needs. But if I am always rushing to the next thing, I am never fully present and don't have time to put others first. Slowing down also prevents unnecessary mistakes and the accompanying frustration. As the Navy SEALS say, "Slow is smooth and smooth is fast."

Adding margin is planning ahead to be loving. It allows me to love my family because I am able to be helpful and engaged. Calm is contagious. Poor planning (not leaving early), over planning (too busy), or delayed planning (procrastination) always sets me up for frustration and an unloving attitude. Poor planning on my part does not constitute an emergency for everyone else or the right for me to be unloving. If I fail to plan, I plan to fail. Frustration and an unloving attitude will be close behind.

As important as many tasks are, even more important is how our life is impacting others. If we measure success by how many boxes we check on our to-do list, we will always be frustrated when others interrupt our all-important task. In the words of my friend and fellow missionary, Steve Stairs: "Margin can often be accomplished by ordering our efficiency around impacting people rather than accomplishing tasks." If our priority is to love others, we will create the time and space to make that happen!

> "So whoever knows the right thing to do and fails to do it, for him it is sin" (James 4:17).

6. Am I forgiving others in love?

When I don't forgive, it is an unloving heart that is clinging to bitterness, resentment, or wounded pride. This allows past events to influence my love for others today. In his book *Anatomy of the Soul*, Curt Thompson, M.D., writes: "Your brain activity . . . is taking place only in the present moment. There is no 'past' as such inherent in this activity. This is important, given how much weight many people give to what they perceive as the past, as if it were an objective reality apart from what their brains are constructing in the present moment. So while you may have viewed the events of your life story as if they were irrevocably chiseled in granite, you have more power than you thought."[24] Our past doesn't affect us. Rather, our current thoughts about the past are what affect us! While we cannot change the past, we can change our thoughts about past events. Finding freedom from those thoughts begins with forgiveness.

John MacArthur says: "I am convinced that multitudes of Christians who suffer from stress, depression, discouragement, relationship problems, and all sorts of other hardships experience these things because of a refusal to forgive."[25] Unwillingness to forgive will leave us spring-loaded for frustration. If little things frustrate us, it may be because, below the surface, there's something we haven't forgiven. Chances are the person you are struggling to forgive doesn't even realize something is bothering you. When frustration bubbles to the top, something is under the surface. Figure out the deeper reason. Forgiving others is a result of love as we release the past, freeing us to love in the present.

In ministry you will have many opportunities to forgive others and let things go. We are all sinful people and do things that hurt each other, intentionally or unintentionally. We shouldn't be shocked when it happens. My professor Kelly O'Rear used to say, "If you work with sheep, don't be surprised when you step in sheep poop." When you do, show love and forgiveness. Don't hold onto bitterness or anger.

> "For if you forgive others their trespasses, your heavenly Father will also forgive you, but if you do not forgive others their trespasses, neither will your Father forgive your trespasses" (Matthew 6:14, 15).

7. Is my body language and tone of voice loving?

I am learning to use my body as a red flag to warn me when I am frustrated or unloving.

Our body language is an unfiltered view of our heart. Our body shows what we are thinking. We may grit our teeth, clench our jaw or fists, roll our eyes, flare our nostrils, exhale in exasperation, or cross our arms—these are all signs of what is going on inside. If you are like me and are naturally inept at identifying body language, read a couple of good books on this subject. For me, this was like learning a new language to better understand myself and others.

Our tone of voice can also be a more true indication of our heart than our actual words. Our words may be slow and steady, but they can drip with irritation or sarcasm. That is our true heart being revealed. We try to mask our heart with the right words, but our frustration leaks out.

When I finally recognized that my body language and tone of voice were an accurate picture of my heart, I began to take them very seriously. Even if I wasn't outwardly yelling at someone, I still needed to address my heart. Emotions like frustration come out in our body language, and if we can identify them quickly, we can seek God's help. When our heart is unloving, our body language and tone of voice will show it.

"Whoever winks his eyes plans dishonest things; he who purses his lips brings evil to pass" (Proverbs 16:30).

8. Am I taking a deep breath and being slow to speak?

If I'm angry or frustrated, it is better to talk to God first rather than burning bridges with unloving words (spoken or written). Waiting to send an email or having someone proofread it can save me from saying something I may regret.

Our unloving heart can affect our brain and body by triggering emotions. Some of these emotions like anger or fear can actually shut down our brain's ability to think well. From *Anatomy of the Soul*:

> "The sympathetic system activates the body's readiness for defensive action, functioning like an accelerator. When put into motion it raises blood pressure, increases pulse and breathing rates, and tenses muscles. It is what we term the fight-flight mechanism of the body. By contrast, the parasympathetic system acts as the brakes, slowing and calming the body by decreasing blood pressure, slowing heart and breathing rates, and relaxing the body muscles . . . The more we understand the role of such systems, the more actively we can regulate them. For example, if I am aware that my fear is deeply connected to my breathing and heart rate, I can reduce my fear simply by consciously breathing deeply and slowly whenever I sense myself becoming fearful."[26]

When we go into fight or flight mode, the part of the brain we use for decision-making switches from the neocortex (our rational thinking brain) to the parts of our brain meant to deal with life and death emergencies. These parts of our brain lack tact and will get us in trouble if we let them control our actions. When something happens to us which causes a negative emotion, if we don't know how to regulate our emotions they can spiral out of control.

How can our breathing help? We can't consciously control our heart rate or blood pressure. However, we can control our breathing. The book *Emotional Intelligence 2.0* says, "Breathing right [is] one of the simplest yet most powerful techniques that you have at your disposal to manage your emotions . . . making yourself breathe right calms you down and makes you feel better by powering up your rational brain."[27] By slowing down our breathing we are able to affect other parts of our autonomic body systems like lowering heart rate and blood pressure. In doing this we send the signal to our brain that there is no emergency, and we can continue using our neocortex for decision-making. Slowing down to control our body helps control our brain.

These may seem trivial at first, but we have all been in a meeting or conversation when someone said something in anger or their body language or tone of voice was unloving. This destroys trust. If you are on a ministry or missionary team, when people can't control their emotions it creates disunity. Instead of having energy to put into forward momentum to spread the gospel, our energy goes sideways into repairing and managing fragile relationships. It's the difference between rowing a boat and repairing a boat. You don't make much progress when you are repairing holes that someone is actively creating. Be careful that you are not the one creating holes! When someone does or says something that causes your blood pressure to rise, slow your breathing down. This slows your heart rate down. Don't let emotions hijack your responses.

> "Let every person be quick to hear, slow to speak, slow to anger; for the anger of man does not produce the righteousness of God" (James 1:19, 20).

Our love is a vital part of overflowing to others. These ways of evaluating our heart and life can help you know when your heart is being unloving. When you identify an unloving heart, turn to God. Ask Him to fill you with His love so you can overflow to others!

THE BIG PICTURE

Joy that fills our heart will overflow in actions of love. When we put others first, it makes God look great. When we sacrificially give of our life, time, and resources to others, it makes God look satisfying. This is why God loves to use those who are loving—it magnifies Him.

To be used by God, love must permeate all we do. Even when we are not speaking, our love is communicating (or not), for "God is love" (1 John 4:8). Our life of love validates our message of love. Without a life of love no one will listen to our message.

His love must overflow to others.

Chapter 14

OVERFLOWING MESSAGE

*Do I make disciples with loving
yet unashamed boldness?*

*"For if I preach the gospel, that gives me no ground
for boasting. For necessity is laid upon me. Woe to me
if I do not preach the gospel!"* (1 CORINTHIANS 9:16)

WHAT IS OUR MESSAGE?

As servants of God, Christians are messengers. God has entrusted His servants with a message to speak: the Gospel of Jesus Christ. This message is not only for pastors and missionaries, it is for all Christians.

"Go therefore and make disciples of all nations, baptizing them in the name of the Father and of the Son and of the Holy Spirit, teaching them to observe all that I have commanded you. And behold, I am with you always, to the end of the age" (Matthew 28:19, 20).

"You are the salt of the earth, but if salt has lost its taste, how shall its saltiness be restored? It is no longer good for anything except to be thrown out and trampled under people's feet. You are the light of the world. A city set on a hill cannot be hidden. Nor do people light a lamp and put it under a basket, but on a stand, and it gives light to all in the house. In the same way, let your light shine before others, so that they may see your good works and give glory to your Father who is in heaven" (Matthew 5:13-16).

No servant is exempt from this duty. God entrusts some with a greater responsibility, but all are to be faithful with their role.

"He who plants and he who waters are one, and each will receive his wages according to his labor. For we are God's fellow workers" (1 Corinthians 3:8, 9).

As servants we are to be bold and unashamed in speaking the gospel. We are to plant gospel seeds as "God's fellow workers." Who we are is more important than what we do, but what we do is also important. It's more than important; it is essential.

Who we are is the first step. The reason that who we are is more important is because if our life contradicts our message, the message is destroyed. For others to take our message seriously, our life must validate that message. The messenger's life validates it, but the message must be proclaimed.

Without the message, the messenger cannot fulfill their duty.

If our life is going to be an oasis, it needs to bring God's life-giving water to others by sharing the life-giving message. His words are the water of life. Jesus said, "The water that I will give him will become in him a spring of water welling up to eternal life . . . the words that I have spoken to you are spirit and life" (John 6:14, 63). Without the message, there is no oasis!

WHY DOES SHARING THE MESSAGE MATTER TO US?

1. Sharing the message is necessary to please God.

It is possible to serve in a way that doesn't please God. Part of pleasing God is being a faithful messenger. It's speaking the words He gives us to speak. It is speaking truth. Notice how in these verses pleasing God is connected to our speaking.

"But though we had already suffered and been shamefully treated at Philippi, as you know, we had boldness in our God to declare to you the gospel of God in the midst of much conflict. For our appeal does not spring from error or impurity or any attempt to deceive, but just as we have been approved by God to be entrusted with the gospel, *so we speak, not to please man, but to please God who tests our hearts*" (1 Thessalonians 2:2-4).

Who rules our heart?

The litmus test of who rules our heart is this: Who do we seek to please, men or God?

To seek to please others and gain their approval is to value acceptance and the praise of men in this life. To seek to please God and gain His approval is to value acceptance and the praise of God in the future. One of the key ways that shows who we are trying to please is revealed by what we talk about. If we are trying to please people instead of God, we will be less bold in sharing the message of the gospel. Jesus spoke these sobering words: "So everyone who acknowledges me before men, I also will acknowledge before my Father who is in heaven, but whoever denies me before men, I also will deny before my Father who is in heaven" (Matthew 10:32, 33).

The task of the servant is to speak. The messenger must deliver the message.

When caring for HIV-positive patients in South Africa, our primary goal was to share the gospel because it was what people needed most. To care for them physically but ignore their spiritual need would be unloving. Consider this illustration: A patient comes to a doctor because of a bad cut. As the doctor treats the patient they do some tests which reveal cancer. If the doctor treats the patient's felt need of the cut but doesn't tell them about the cancer, we would say the doctor is unloving and not fulfilling his or her duty. Love doesn't neglect people's greatest need. The same is true of us. If we do not speak the message we do not fulfill our duty or show love.

We are sent with the message of eternal life. If we obey God in many areas, but do not obey Him in speaking the message, we are not pleasing to Him. We also bypass reward.

2. Our reward is based on how we fulfill our stewardship.

Delivering the message is our task. If we long for a "well done," then we need to be faithful in the task. If we long for eternal reward, then sharing the message is an essential part. Every conversation is an opportunity to plant gospel seeds that God may choose to grow!

This is so important it is mentioned repeatedly in God's Word.

"His master said to him, 'Well done, good and faithful servant. *You have been faithful over a little; I will set you over much.* Enter into the joy of your master'" (Matthew 25:21).

"For if I preach the gospel, that gives me no ground for boasting. For necessity is laid upon me. Woe to me if I do not preach the gospel! *For if I do this of my own will, I have a reward,* but if not of my own will, I am still entrusted with a stewardship" (1 Corinthians 9:16, 17).

"He who plants and he who waters are one, and *each will receive his wages according to his labor*" (1 Corinthians 3:8).

"And those who are wise shall shine like the brightness of the sky above; and *those who turn many to righteousness, like the stars forever and ever*" (Daniel 12:3).

How are we doing with stewarding the gospel? Are we being faithful to spread it and invest it so it multiples? Or are we burying it, keeping it to ourselves?

God's "well done" goes to those who multiply the stewardship of the gospel by spreading it to others. Don't bury the gospel!

WHY DOES SHARING THE MESSAGE MATTER TO GOD?

What if a servant was responsible to speak the king's words to others but didn't do as he was asked? Instead, the servant lived like a normal citizen of land. No one knew the servant was the king's ambassador because the servant didn't tell anyone. The servant's conversations were no different than those of other people.

Would this servant please the king? Of course not. The servant didn't fulfill his duty as a messenger and ambassador.

Our speaking is important to God because it shows that, as servants, we're unashamed of God. The ashamed, silent servant shows that God is not great or valuable. We are ashamed when we think someone will not like what we have to say. If the servant doesn't speak, he is valuing the listener's opinion, not God's. When the servant is ashamed, he exchanges the approval of God for the approval of men. He would rather please people than God.

Not speaking the message is evidence of a much deeper problem: an unsubmitted heart. When the heart seeks to please another master, we are actually benefiting the rebel leader, Satan.

Why would a king send a messenger who will not boldly proclaim his message?

Silent messengers are not messengers. Silent messengers trade future reward for current reward. They seek the peace and leisure of not having to speak the message and going against what is culturally acceptable. They seek the approval of others as they conform to the standard of others.

As messengers and ambassadors, we carry God's words to others. "We are ambassadors for Christ, God making his appeal through us" (2 Corinthians 5:20).

If we are not speaking the message, we are not pleasing God!

HOW DO WE GROW IN BOLDNESS?

1. Depend on the power of the Holy Spirit.

Boldness is not something I can muster on my own; it must come from God.

> *"For God gave us a spirit not of fear but of power* and love and self-control. *Therefore do not be ashamed* of the testimony about our Lord, nor of me his prisoner, but share in suffering for the gospel by the power of God" (2 Timothy 1:7, 8).

> "But you will receive power *when the Holy Spirit has come upon you,* and *you will be my witnesses* in Jerusalem and in all Judea and Samaria, and to the end of the earth" (Acts 1:8).

> "And now, Lord, look upon their threats and *grant to your servants to continue to speak your word with all boldness,* while you stretch out your hand to heal, and signs and wonders are performed through the name of your holy servant Jesus. And when they had prayed, the place in which *they were gathered together was shaken, and they were all filled with the Holy Spirit and continued to speak the word of God with boldness"* (Acts 4:29-31).

Even though I don't have the power in myself to muster boldness, I can pray for more boldness. And as I step out in faith like the priests into the Jordan River, God will grant me the boldness I need. But I must take those steps of faith. I must open my mouth and start conversations about God and the gospel.

Not only is God the source of biblical boldness, but boldness also points people to God. My friend Steve Stairs has said, "biblical boldness does not attract attention to the one having it. The boldness we see in our world does exactly that. Biblical boldness is the courage to speak and do what should be said and done at just the right time. For example, when Jerusalem was in an uproar over the sound that filled the city and seemingly ignorant people speaking in languages they never studied, Peter stood up and spoke a message that explained what God was doing. Biblical boldness always speaks and acts for God so that God will be noticed and understood."

2. Spend much time in worship.

We all look for opportunities to talk about the things we enjoy. The mouth praises what the heart loves. If I have a hard time talking about God before others, my personal delight and worship of Him may be too small. If I always talk about other things, then maybe I love those other things more than God! What do I talk about most? I talk about what I love. If my words reveal that my love of God is small, I need to spend more time in worship.

> "May all who seek you rejoice and be glad in you; may those who love your salvation say continually, 'Great is the Lord!'" (Psalm 40:16)

3. Be unashamed of God and the message.

"*So have no fear of them,* for nothing is covered that will not be revealed, or hidden that will not be known. What I tell you in the dark, say in the light, and what you hear whispered, proclaim on the housetops. And do not fear those who kill the body but cannot kill the soul. Rather fear him who can destroy both soul and body in hell. Are not two sparrows sold for a penny? And not one of them will fall to the ground apart from your Father. But even the hairs of your head are all numbered. Fear not, therefore; you are of more value than many sparrows. *So everyone who acknowledges me before men, also will acknowledge before my Father who is in heaven, but whoever denies me before men, I also will deny before my Father who is in heaven"* (Matthew 10:26-33).

It can be fearful to speak God's Word to others. But I must always remember that if they reject the message, they're rejecting God, not me. Whenever it feels like people are rejecting me, God reminds me of His encouragement to Samuel: "They have not rejected you, but they have rejected me from being king over them" (1 Samuel 8:7). Better to please my Master who I will be with forever than to please others for a moment.

4. Have faith in God to bring about His future promises.

Boldness is built on hope and faith. I can be bold because I am confident that what I say is true. Boldness is an outward evidence of inner faith. If I lack faith, I will lack boldness.

> " . . . for which I was appointed a preacher and apostle and teacher, which is why I suffer as I do. But I am not ashamed, for I know whom I have believed, and I am convinced that he is able to guard until that Day what has been entrusted to me" (2 Timothy 1:11, 12).

"For I am not ashamed of the gospel, for it is the power of God for salvation to everyone who believes, to the Jew first and also to the Greek" (Romans 1:16).

"Since we have such a hope, we are very bold" (2 Corinthians 3:12).

If this world is all there is, there are no grounds for any boldness. But if my eternity is secure and God's view of me is the only view that matters, I can be bold before others and unashamed of the message. My focus must stay on God's promises!

5. Obey God's command to speak the message.

"But Peter and the apostles answered, '*We must obey God* rather than men'" (Acts 5:29).

Even when I don't feel bold and brave, I can still obey. Speaking to others to share the hope of the gospel is part of obedience. To overlook this command means I am much more like a stagnant pond, not an overflowing stream. His Word must be flowing through me to others.

6. Be confident that God will use the message to save unbelievers.

"Therefore I endure everything for the sake of the elect, *that they also may obtain the salvation* that is in Christ Jesus with eternal glory" (2 Timothy 2:10).

I don't depend on my method or delivery of the gospel to save others, I depend on the power of the Holy Spirit to awaken new life. True change in others depends on God, not me. I am responsible to share, but God draws people to Himself.

"What then is Apollos? What is Paul? Servants through whom you believed, as the Lord assigned to each. I planted, Apollos watered, but God gave the growth. So neither he who plants nor he who waters is anything, but only God who gives the growth" (1 Corinthians 3:5-7).

I plant the seeds, God causes the growth. This removes the burden of results from me. This truth is essential to cling to: *the results are in God's hands.* God encouraged Paul with these words: "Do not be afraid, but go on speaking and do not be silent, for I am with you, and no one will attack you to harm you, for *I have many in this city who are my people*" (Acts 18:9, 10). God calls them "my people" even before Paul preached the gospel to them. God doesn't always guarantee our safety, but He does guarantee the salvation of "my people." My role is to plant the seeds, God's role is to grow them. I can rest in God's power to change hearts!

It is vital that we rest in God's power to save and not in our ability as a messenger or in the hearer's ability to respond to the message. Why? Because the glory of God is at stake. As God's messengers, our pride is tempted to embezzle just a little bit of credit for our part when a person believes in Christ as their Savior. As people come to faith in Christ, they are tempted to take a little credit for their ability to believe. Paul reminds us of God's choice so that we would not photobomb God in our preaching, evangelism, or even our own salvation:

"For consider your calling, brothers: not many of you were wise according to worldly standards, not many were powerful, not many were of noble birth. But God chose what is foolish in the world to shame the wise; God chose what is weak in the world to shame the strong; God chose what is low and despised in the world, even things that are not, to bring to nothing things that are, so that no human being might boast in the presence of God. And because of him you are in Christ Jesus, who became to us wisdom from God, righteousness and sanctification and redemption, so that, as it is written, 'Let the one who boasts, boast in the Lord'" (1 Corinthians 1:26-31).

God alone deserves the glory! This truth of God's choice gives us boldness as we rest in His power and gives Him all the glory. We have nothing to fear and nothing to boast of.

God gave me many opportunities that tested my boldness to proclaim Christ in South Africa. One of the most memorable was my first time preaching in Zulu to a large group. A Zulu pastor friend asked me if I would speak at a ceremony for the "induna," the Zulu word for local chief. One week before the ceremony, the pastor asked how my preparation was coming for the ceremony for the "inkosi." The word "inkosi" means the area king. I replied, "You said the 'induna,' not the 'inkosi.' Which one is it?" He replied, "Sorry, I meant the inkosi." I almost dropped the phone. "How many people do you think will be there?" I asked. "Probably about five hundred," he replied. I almost dropped the phone again.

This was not my idea of easing into preaching in Zulu. My vocabulary was still limited, so I was only able to preach with the eloquence of a six-year-old. But this forced me to rely on the power of God, not my eloquence. On the day of the event about 300 people were there. Among them were many ancestor worshipers, Zionists, and Shembe worshipers, all groups whose beliefs opposed Jesus as the only way of salvation. God is faithful. He gave the boldness and courage to speak truth. I took courage in the fact that the message wasn't mine, it was God's. I was simply sharing truth from God's authoritative Word. Not only was the message God's, the results were His also. My role was to be the messenger by planting seeds of the gospel. God's role was to grow them.

When we rest on God and His Word, we find the boldness to be God's messengers.

STARTING GOSPEL CONVERSATIONS

Sometimes during a conversation there is a natural opening for a clear and bold gospel presentation. Do you ever find it hard to start these conversations?

Most evangelism tools assume you are already in a conversation with someone. These tools help us clearly present the gospel, but they rarely help us start conversations.

Here are a few tips I've found helpful for starting conversations that naturally lead to the gospel. Most are from the books *Sent*, by Ashley and Heather Holleman, and *God Space*, by Doug Pollock. I highly recommend both books.

See people as Jesus does

Gospel conversations happen from simply seeing people the way Jesus does. We need to slow down enough to care for them as a person. When people feel you truly care, it opens doors to deeper conversations. Make this your daily prayer: "Lord, help me see others as you do."

Smile

Smiling is a visible way to show our joy in God and love for others. The power of a smile is often overlooked but is impactful anywhere in the world. A smile shows you are friendly and approachable—something people look for when starting conversations.

Find something to comment on

We can comment on something we have in common, like shared experiences, shared interests, the weather, and more. We can notice something the other person enjoys and use it as a conversations starter (pets, hobbies, etc.). We can also notice something to genuinely compliment a person on. What we say doesn't have to be earth-shattering, just something to break the ice. Finding common ground is easiest when we are involved in activities and hobbies with unbelievers. Like Jesus, we should be a friend of sinners.

Ask open questions about the other person

Be curious! Being curious helps us ask deeper questions, and often they are questions people love to answer. Most people love to talk about themselves and things they find interesting—asking questions shows we care about them as a person. "Let each of you look not only to his own interests, but also to the interests of others" (Philippians 2:4).

Most people will mention, often in passing, the things they love or want to talk about. As people tell you about themselves, try to actively listen and ask follow-up questions. Using open questions promotes good conversation because they take some explanation on the other person's part and cannot be answered with a simple yes or no.

Examples:

"What made you want to become a ____?"

"Why do you enjoy ____?"

Look for open doors to plant gospel seeds

As we talk with people, notice opportunities for deeper spiritual questions or comments. This doesn't mean noticing opportunities to monologue a gospel presentation! Our goal is to talk with the person, not at them. The goal is deeper dialogue. Actively listening and staying curious creates a safe place for people to share their true selves. When they do, they may share specific needs, concerns, or questions that need God's help. They may also share hopes, dreams, and values that reveal their deepest longings. All of these open doors to point people to God. Pray that God will "open to us a door for the word, to declare the mystery of Christ" (Colossians 4:3). I use a daily reminder on my phone, at 4:03 pm, to pray for open doors!

Here are four ways to plant gospel seeds.

1. Mention God, prayer, and the Bible in the conversation

Just talk about God as a natural part of everyday life.

2. Quote or paraphrase the Bible

Look for opportunities to use the phrase: *"What you're saying reminds me of something I read in the Bible, where God says* _____ *."*[28]

3. Use questions

Here are a few helpful questions.

"What does your tradition say about Jesus?"

"Do you consider yourself on a spiritual journey? What's that like? Where are you on that journey?"

"I'm in a fresh season of prayer. Do you have any prayer requests I might commit to pray for?"

"Can I tell you something I just learned in the Bible that's changing how I handle _____ *?"*[29]

After one of these questions, you can then start to ask about Jesus:

"You can probably tell I'm a Christian and someone who studies the Bible. Do you have any questions about Jesus I could try to answer for you?"[30]

This gives people an open invitation to ask anything they're curious about! For more examples of great questions, check out *God Space*, referenced above.

Questions like these are helpful in many contexts, but there is no one-size-fits-all question. The best questions are those that come from actively listening and staying curious. When we listen and form our questions based on what people have said, the questions will naturally fit the conversation.

4. Share stories

When fitting, share a brief story of how God has worked in your life: your salvation story, an example of personal surrender, or a story of answered prayer. Close the story with a Bible verse that highlights God's work in the story. Stories are helpful, but only God's Word is powerful enough to lead to salvation.

Invite a response

Not every conversation has to include a gospel presentation or invitation to respond. People may need to believe foundational truths like the existence of God before they're ready for a gospel presentation or a full response. Starting conversations can create a safe space to discuss spiritual things and plant seeds of truth. As Jesus said, "One sows and another reaps" (John 4:37).

When do we move from explaining how to know God personally to inviting someone to respond? Wait for the leading of the Holy Spirit. When He leads, we can ask:

"What about you? Who do you believe Jesus is?"

If God doesn't lead in this way, invite them to continue the conversation or study the Bible. Say something like:

"I enjoyed this conversation. Would you like to talk more about this another time?"

"I would love to talk more about this. Would you like to get together to look at what the Bible has to say?"

Keep building deeper relationships and deeper connections to God's Word. Be bold to start conversations and look for open doors for the gospel! God's "well done" goes to those who steward the gospel well by spreading it to others . . . one conversation at a time.

MULTIPLY

As we make disciples of Jesus Christ, our goal is to make disciples who make disciples. Our goal is to multiply. Even though sometimes we have the opportunity to share Christ to larger numbers of people, equipping individuals to multiply often yields greater long-term results.

> "Other seeds fell on good soil and produced grain, some a hundredfold, some sixty, some thirty" (Matthew 13:8).

We want to bear much fruit. Jesus said, "Whoever abides in me and I in him, he it is that bears much fruit, for apart from me you can do nothing" (John 15:5).

The essential factor in bearing much fruit is the power of God to spread the gospel and change hearts. Strategy alone in disciple-making will yield nothing because, apart from God, we can do nothing. All our labor is done in the strength He supplies.

However, we do have a role. Though I've presented it before, this verse is so key:

> "Go therefore and make disciples of all nations, baptizing them in the name of the Father and of the Son and of the Holy Spirit, *teaching them to observe all that I have commanded you.* And behold, I am with you always, to the end of the age" (Matthew 28:19, 20).

Part of what we teach and equip disciples to obey is the command to make new disciples. We teach and equip others to multiply.

Our goal is to see God glorified by multiplying disciples who God grows into churches. We long to see this happen, and everything we do is meant to help this goal. Yet even with that goal, I have unknowingly done things that hinder multiplication. I have done things that were good, but not best.

God still used those things to make disciples, but I realized there were things I did that hindered multiplication. This is not to say that God cannot and does not overcome those hindrances. I didn't stop God's plan. But just as in our personal spiritual life, I want to remove any hindrances and barriers to allow the power of God to flow freely. I want to get out of the way.

This phrase has become one of my mantras: Simplify to multiply.

Simple things multiply well. If things become too complex, multiplication is harder.

By simplify, I do not mean dumbing down what we teach or how we train. Simplify means removing the clutter.

The first barrier to multiplication is us. We can't do all the work. Each disciple must be equipped to multiply. That is task number one. If we don't equip others to multiply, then we must do all the work. If every disciple is equipped to multiply, the reach of the gospel multiplies incredibly. Even though Jesus had a ministry to the multitudes, His primary ministry was to His disciples. He poured His life into a few men, and those men did the same to others. Jesus practiced life-on-life discipleship.

If Jesus' primary focus was on discipling people deeply, I believe it is best for us to do this as well.

My focus must be on people, not programs. I must simplify my focus on programs to focus on people. It's easy to think that bigger is better, but numbers are not the goal. Deep disciples who multiply deep disciples is the goal. This will result in numbers, but of a very different type of disciple. In the long run, deep disciples who multiply will yield a greater harvest than many shallow Christians who do not multiply.

Paul understood this truth. He told Timothy, "What you have heard from me in the presence of many witnesses entrust to faithful men, who will be able to teach others also" (2 Timothy 2:2). There are four generations of believers listed here: Paul, Timothy, faithful men, and others. That's how we multiply. We pour into others and equip them to multiply. By simplifying to multiply we can focus our energy in the right areas so we are not spread too thin. Multiplying disciples isn't as glamorous as multiplying programs, but it yields better and more long-term results.

How am I doing in equipping others to multiply? Am I focusing on people or programs?

Jesus had a ministry to the multitudes, but His primary work was with a few disciples. He made disciples that made disciples. He multiplied. If Jesus made this His primary work, so can I. So can you.

A second barrier to multiplication is the method and materials we use to train others. Some ways that we train and equip people may work well for a first generation church but are not designed to multiply into a fourth generation church. As I reflect on our time in South Africa, I often didn't use materials that were simple enough to multiply. If each of the people I taught wanted to share beyond their immediate family, finances and materials often were the bottleneck. If evangelism materials are too complicated and expensive to reproduce, then I am unintentionally hindering multiplication.

When we equip disciples, let's resource them to share the hope of the gospel with materials and methods that are simple enough to reproduce. Simplify to multiply. This is not a call to eliminate seminaries or dumb down education. This is a focus on equipping each disciple to multiply disciples. Get disciples grounded in the Word by teaching them *how to study it for themselves and how to share it with others*. If our disciples don't have a method to study and share God's Word, they will always be dependent on more resources. They will always be dependent on more finances for those resources. Resources aren't bad, but the resources we use to spread the gospel should be easy to multiply.

This desire to remove barriers to multiplication led me to create Discover God, an evangelistic tool to multiply disciples. If you don't have a simple, reproducible tool to multiply disciples, you can find it here: https://global.liveglobal.org/resource/discover-god/ .

It is 100 percent free to use, reproduce, and translate.

I pray that God will use it to help you make disciples who make disciples!

THE BIG PICTURE

Do we desire to see God glorified through our lives? Then we must speak the message!

We need to let God overflow from our lives in our joy, love, and words. We can't keep it to ourselves; it needs to be shared!

Like our joy and love, the message must overflow from us. As God's words flow into us, they will flow out of us. What is in your heart will overflow. "Out of the abundance of the heart the mouth speaks" (Luke 6:45).

God sends us to the desert where we are surrounded by lost people who will die in their sins unless they receive the life-giving water of God. They must trust in Jesus Christ to find salvation, for "there is salvation in no one else, for there is no other name under heaven given among men by which we must be saved" (Acts 4:12). Jesus said, "I am the way, and the truth, and the life. No one comes to the Father except through me" (John 14:6).

To believe, others must hear the message.

"'For everyone who calls on the name of the Lord will be saved.' How then will they call on him in whom they have not believed? And how are they to believe in him of whom they have never heard? And *how are they to hear without someone preaching*? And how are they to preach unless they are sent? As it is written, 'How beautiful are the feet of those who preach the good news!'" (Romans 10:13-15).

Servants who are pleasing and useful to God both model the message and share the message.

I am not personally gifted as an evangelist, but my reward isn't based on gifting. It is based on faithfulness. Our "well done" is contingent on how faithful we are in sharing the message! Are you faithfully sharing?

May our life be continually overflowing so we can share the life-giving water of the gospel with a dying world.

Without the message, there is no oasis!

Conclusion

NOW WHAT?

Like water, God is searching for servants with no barriers who are connected to Him. He is waiting to flow through you with His power and overflow from you to a world in desperate need.

EVALUATE YOURSELF

When God searches your heart, what does He find?

Does He find a heart aligned to His plan and seeking His glory alone, or one that's embezzling glory?

Does He find a heart like David's, one that loves Him fully and seeks after Him with a whole heart, or does He find someone who has lost their awe of God?

Does He find a heart committed and submitted to Him in obedience, or does He find the barriers of sin hindering the flow of His power?

Does He find a heart that overflows to others like a desert oasis, freely sharing the love and message of Christ, or does He find grace hoarders that keep the good news to themselves?

PURSUE USEFULNESS

Do you want to be used by God?

God's plan will never be hindered or stopped. It will happen as He planned. But as God works, He is searching for the right kind of servant to bring about His plan.

Do we have a part in being useful to God and the success of our ministry or life? Yes, but it is not based in our ability. It is in our trust and obedience, faith and holiness. When God spoke to Joshua, He told him to do two things: trust without fear, and obey His commands.

> "*Be strong and courageous,* for you shall cause this people to inherit the land that I swore to their fathers to give them. Only *be strong and very courageous, being careful to do according to all the law that Moses my servant commanded you. Do not turn from it to the right hand or to the left,* that you may have good success wherever you go. *This Book of the Law shall not depart from your mouth, but you shall meditate on it day and night, so that you may be careful to do according to all that is written in it.* For then you will make your way prosperous, and then you will have good success. Have I not commanded you? *Be strong and courageous. Do not be frightened, and do not be dismayed,* for the Lord your God is with you wherever you go" (Joshua 1:6-9).

Remember the contingent promises God gave Joshua. If Joshua would trust God and obey His commands, *then* he would have good success.

"*For* you shall cause this people to inherit the land" (v. 6).

"*That* you may have good success wherever you go" (v. 7).

"*For then* you will make your way prosperous, and then you will have good success" (v. 8).

You do have a part in making your way prosperous and finding success: stay connected to God and allow Him to push out the barriers of sin. Trust and obey.

Success is a gift from God, but He loves to give it to those who follow and honor Him with their whole heart. Success is being used by God to bring about His plan to glorify Himself. Our plans may fail, but God's never do.

God wants servants who are useful and pleasing to Him, servants after His own heart. As God's children, each of us has the opportunity to be one to whom God looks! Each of us could be a servant who receives God's strong support as we serve!

Who you are is more important than what you do, because what you do flows out of who you are. What you do is important, but your heart is more important. If the source is sweet, the actions and words will be sweet as well.

When God searches for people to use He is not looking at abilities or accomplishments. His power alone can accomplish the spiritual work He desires. He is searching for hearts He can use to flow through unhindered. Right now, God is searching for useful hearts to glorify His greatness. When He finds these hearts He pours out His strong support, using them to magnify His name before a world in need of its king. At the end of this age, these servants will hear their Master speak the precious words: "Well done, good and faithful servant"!

Reward and success are contingent on *hard* work (Colossians 3:23, 24), but even more importantly, *heart* work.

God is looking at *your* heart. Will He find a useful heart?

You grow in usefulness as your heart becomes filled to overflowing. Align your life to God, the Spring of life, by living for His glory alone. Like a stream, connect to God in worship. Ask God to push the barriers of sin out of your heart so He can freely flow through you. Connect to others so that God's love and message overflows from you like a desert oasis.

My prayer for you is this: That you would *be* who God wants you to be, so you can *do* what God wants you to do. Day in and day out, no matter what, we need to *be* a disciple who *makes* disciple makers.

May you be filled to overflowing!

"The eyes of the Lord run to and fro throughout the whole earth, to give strong support to those whose heart is blameless toward him" (2 Chronicles 16:9).

Appendix

OVERFLOWING HEALTH

Am I maximizing my physical health to maximize my long-term spiritual usefulness?

"His master said to him, 'Well done, good and faithful servant. You have been faithful over a little; I will set you over much. Enter into the joy of your master'" (Matthew 25:21).

HEALTHY VESSELS

Does my health matter? Does my physical health affect my long-term usefulness?

I believe it does.

Working to improve our health has temporal and eternal ramifications. Let's look at both.

Temporal Ramifications

Over the past decade I have faced many health issues:

- Debilitating lower back pain that made meetings and travel unbearable

- Sciatica

- Weight gain from furlough and travel

- Rosacea and eczema (minor life problem, but indicative of internal inflammation)

- Irritable bowel syndrome from food sensitivities

- Debilitating migraines from stress

- Sports injuries

- Difficulty sleeping

- Allergies

- Joint pain

Each of these has affected my ability to minister well. One by one, God allowed me to find solutions to remove or manage the problems. This has opened ministry opportunities that were previously not possible because of health problems. As we ask ourselves this question—"What else could I do to improve my health?"—we may find health solutions that enable extra years of life and ministry.

Eternal Ramifications

God is sovereign over all things, including our health. He can take health away in the blink of an eye, but we are responsible to do what is wise and best. He gave each of us a body to steward the best we can. We will have to give an account of how we used our talents, including how we took care of our body.

All of my mentors and role models have worked to maintain their health. Their example has been inspiring. I borrowed my first weights from Bob Kennel when I was 13. Don Trott exercised regularly and ate well, despite crazy travels. Bob Farison is 94 and still preaching weekly! They have worked to maximize their health so they can maximize their longevity and energy in ministry.

If I owned a business and an employee was unable to work because of an unhealthy lifestyle, as an employer I would not say, "Well done." In the same way, if I do things that sabotage my health and affect my ability to minister, those choices will affect my eternal "well done." I want to do everything I can to live in a healthy way so I can serve the Lord as long as possible. This does not refer to the instances of unavoidable illness or disease that God allows. It does refer to poor health I bring upon myself through neglect or bad choices. It also refers to illness I bring upon myself because of chronic worry, hurry, or unforgiveness. If I live in a state of chronic stress, my body goes into survival mode and not repair mode. If my immune system is weak because I don't do the things I should, it makes me more susceptible to illnesses. If I know the right thing to do, will I do it? What will I value more? The "well done," or living, temporarily, how I want? I can't hide behind my belief in the sovereignty of God as an excuse to treat my body poorly.

I want to finish well. I want to hear "well done, good and faithful servant." If the Lord wills, I want to keep ministering in some way long past normal retirement age. If my body is going to last that long, I need to make adjustments now. I want to be faithful to do my part by removing things that sabotage my health and adding things that improve longevity.

WANT TO DIVE DEEPER?

You probably already have a fairly good idea of where to start with improving your health through diet and exercise. Or, such programs can easily be found. I encourage you to start right away with the obvious changes.

If you want optimal health, it's going to take dedication. Over the last twenty years I have studied and experimented with different diets and exercise plans to find what works best. Recently, I put what I learned into some evaluation tools that can be used to identify areas of weakness.

Hopefully, these tools will save months or even years of your own personal self-experimentation!

Blog Post:
https://www.kylefarran.com/Achilles-Strength

Evaluation Tool:
https://www.kylefarran.com/Achilles-Strength-Evaluation-Tool

I pray these thoughts and tools will aid you on your journey as you seek to serve the Master and remain useful to Him for many years to come!

May we each hear "well done" for keeping a healthy heart, both spiritually and physically.

Acknowledgments

This book has taken a decade to complete. Without the help of many people, it would still be an unpublished file on my computer. I am deeply grateful to the following people.

Thank you to my wife, Heather. Your support and encouragement have been so critical. Your questions, input, and suggestions have vastly improved the entire book. Thank you for being patient with me while I worked and reworked material. You made this book possible!

Thank you to my children: Abigail, Emily, and Natalie. Abigail and Emily, for helping make edits and giving input on the cover. Emily for taking my profile picture. Natalie, for being patient while I spent extra time writing.

Thank you to my parents and extended family for encouraging me to write. It meant so much to feel your support.

Thank you to Patti McCoy Hummel, who has been an incredible literary agent. You shared your years of experience and helped make this dream a reality.

Thank you to my publishers Shane Crabtree and Larry Carpenter at Carpenter's Son Publishing. You and your team have been a joy to work with and have helped guide me through the publishing process.

Thanks to my many friends who read parts of the book and gave feedback on early drafts: Vic Willis, Ryan Christian, Alex Kocman, Jeff Demerly, Drew Woods, Brad Winkler, Scott Carter, Landon Shuman, Harry Gebert, Sandy Farran, Clint Archer, James Lytle, Keith Hudak, and Don Tinney. Thanks as well to the many others who gave input on the title and subtitle.

Special thanks to Steve Stairs, who took time to give important input from a theological perspective.

Thanks to Bob Irvin, my editor. You did an incredible job taking my thoughts and helping them be clearly communicated.

Thanks to Suzanne Lawing, who helped with the cover design and layout. You did great work, and I appreciate your patience as you tried my many ideas for the cover.

Thanks to Tom Reynolds for helping make this book possible.

Thanks to Clint Archer for writing the foreword.

Thanks to Bill Parsons, who was my coach during the writing process and gave great encouragement.

Thanks to those whose lives have deeply impacted me. My parents, who left everything to go into missions when I was five and modeled what it means to follow God. Thanks to the men whose Christlike example shaped my life: Bob Kennell, Kyle Detmers, Kelly O'Rear, Bob Farison, Drew Woods, Don Trott, and Bruce McDonald.

Finally, my greatest thanks goes to God. The words in this book cannot be attributed to any wisdom in me. If God speaks to your heart through this book, it is because He has first spoken to my heart. I am simply sharing what God has challenged me with. Oceans of glory to God, but to I not a drop.

"For from him and through him and to him are all things. To him be glory forever. Amen" (ROMANS 11:36).

Notes

1. Genesis 6:5; 1 Chronicles 29:18; Psalm 16:9, 37:4, 38:8; Matthew 9:4, 15:19; 1 Corinthians 4:5

2. Message by James Grier: https://soundcloud.com/grand-rapids-theological-seminary/series-10-words-lesson-10-james-grier

3. Elliot, Elisabeth, *Shadow of the Almighty: The Life and Testament of Jim Elliot* (New York, NY: HarperCollins, 1989), p.116.

4. https://en.wikipedia.org/wiki/Okavango_Delta

5. https://whc.unesco.org/en/list/1432/

6. Piper, John, *Don't Waste Your Life* (Wheaton, IL: Crossway, 2003), p. 32.

7. Bridges, Jerry, *The Pursuit of Holiness* (Colorado Springs, CO: Navpress, 2001), pp. 84, 85.

8. Godin, Seth, *Tribes: We Need You to Lead Us* (New York, NY: Penguin Group, 2008), p. 92.

9. Piper, John, https://www.desiringgod.org/messages/
the-god-who-strengthens-his-people-part-2

10. Thompson M.D., Curt, *Anatomy of the Soul: Surprising Connections between Neuroscience and Spiritual Practices That Can Transform Your Life and Relationships* (Tyndale House Publishers, Inc., 2010, Kindle Edition), p. 65.

11. https://positivepsychology.com/neuroscience-of-gratitude/

12. Jocko Willink interview with Tim Ferriss: https://fhww.files.wordpress.com/2018/08/107-jocko-willink.pdf

13. Piper, John, *The Dangerous Duty of Delight* (Sisters, OR: Multnomah, 2001), p. 34.

14. Welch, Suzy, *10/10/10* (New York, NY: Scribner, 2009).

15. Piper, John, Article: "How Do You Define Joy?" https://www.desiringgod.org/articles/how-do-you-define-joy

16. Lewis, C.S., *The Weight of Glory: And Other Addresses* (New York, NY: HarperCollins Publishers, 1949), p. 26.

17. Piper, John, *Desiring God: Meditations of a Christian Hedonist* (Sisters, OR: Multnomah, 2003), p. 288.

18. Edwards, Jonathan, "Miscellanies," in *The Works of Jonathan Edwards, vol. 13*, ed. Thomas Schafer (New Haven, CT: Yale University Press, 1994), p. 495 (miscellany #448).

19. MacArthur, John, Sermon: "Killing the Sin in Your Life," https://www.gty.org/library/sermons-library/81-51/killing-the-sin-in-your-life

20. Carnegie, Dale, *How to Win Friends and Influence People* (Simon & Schuster: Kindle Edition), p. 202.

21. Patterson, Kerry; Grenny, Joseph; McMillan, Ron; Switzler, Al; Maxfield, David. *Crucial Accountability: Tools for Resolving Violated Expectations, Broken Commitments, and Bad Behavior, Second Edition* (McGraw-Hill Education: Kindle Edition), p. 71.

22. Carmichael, Amy. https://quotefancy.com/quote/1494157/ Amy-Carmichael-A-cup-brimful-of-sweetness-cannot-spill-even-one-drop-of-bitter-water-no#:~:text=Amy%20 Carmichael%20Quote%3A%20%E2%80%9CA%20cup,no%20 matter%20how%20suddenly%20jarred.%E2%80%9D

23. Mckeown, Greg, *Essentialism: The Disciplined Pursuit of Less* (The Crown Publishing Group: Kindle Edition), p. 181.

24. Thompson, *Anatomy of the Soul,* pp. 76, 77.

25. MacArthur, John, *The Freedom and Power of Forgiveness* (Wheaton, IL: Crossway, 1998), p. 112.

26. Thompson, pp. 42, 43.

27. Bradberry, Travis; Greaves, Jean. *Emotional Intelligence 2.0* (San Diego, CA: TalentSmart, 2009, Kindle Edition), p. 103.

28. Holleman, Ashley, Holleman, Heather. *Sent: Living a Life That Invites Others to Jesus* (Moody Publishers, Kindle Edition, 2020), p. 65.

29. Holleman, p. 152.

30. Holleman, p. 155.

About the Author

Kyle Farran grew up as a missionary kid and has served overseas as a missionary since 2007. He and his family spent eight years in South Africa opening a HIV/AIDS Hospice Care Home and then training Zulu pastors. Since 2015 he has served as a Regional Director for ABWE, leading and developing missionaries to help them fully live out their calling. He received his Master of Ministry in Organizational Leadership from Clarks Summit University, is a ICF-credentialed life and leadership coach, and is a licensed instructor of The COACH Model®. Kyle and his wife, Heather, have three daughters and live in Lisbon, Portugal.

Find out more at kylefarran.com